Advance Praise for *Your Way Back to Happy*

"Janelle's gift to the world is her ability to communicate knowledge and understanding about a difficult subject like trauma through a soft lens of healing. The title of the book says it all, you can trust Janelle to be your guide on your journey to happiness."

DR. DON WOOD PHD
Founder, Inspired Performance Institute

"For leaders running on empty, *Your Way Back to Happy* offers practical and helpful tools built on trust, purpose, and intentional growth that can help a person move from merely surviving to truly thriving."

STEPHEN M.R. COVEY
The New York Times **and**
#1 *Wall Street Journal* **bestselling author
of** *The Speed of Trust* **and** *Trust & Inspire*

"This short sentence from *Your Way Back to Happy* hit home with me: "Your past can get in the way of your best future." I have worked with thousands of entrepreneurs and leaders and far too often I hear some version of: "I know I was meant for more but every time I feel like I am on the verge of a breakthrough something stops me dead in my tracks - even if I am successful in the moment the voice in the back of my head says it will never last." If this sounds like you then I have good news - this book is *Your Way Back to Happy!*

TOM ZIGLAR
CEO Zig Ziglar Corporation

Your Way Back to Happy

Your Way Back to Happy

How to Turn the Pain of Your Past into a Future of Freedom, Purpose, and Peace

Janelle Bruland

A POST HILL PRESS BOOK
ISBN: 979-8-89565-043-1
ISBN (eBook): 979-8-89565-044-8

Your Way Back to Happy:
How to Turn the Pain of Your Past into a Future of Freedom, Purpose, and Peace
© 2025 by Janelle Bruland
All Rights Reserved

Cover design by Conroy Accord

This book, as well as any other Post Hill Press publications, may be purchased in bulk quantities at a special discounted rate. Contact orders@posthillpress.com for more information.

All people, locations, events, and situations are portrayed to the best of the author's memory. While all of the events described are true, many names and identifying details have been changed to protect the privacy of the people involved.

No part of this book may be reproduced, stored in a retrieval system, or transmitted by any means without the written permission of the author and publisher.

Post Hill Press
New York • Nashville
posthillpress.com

Published in the United States of America
1 2 3 4 5 6 7 8 9 10

Contents

Introduction ix

Part One: Understanding the Problem

Chapter 1: You Look Fine, but You Are Not Fine 3

Chapter 2: Your Trauma Doesn't Need to Be
Your Prison 11

Chapter 3: You Are Not Alone 23

Chapter 4: From Pushing Through to Letting Go 35

Chapter 5: You Have the Power to Take Back
Control of Your Life 50

Part Two: The Practical Application

Chapter 6: Put Your Past in the Past 63

Chapter 7: Your Brain is Lying to You 73

Chapter 8: Get in Tune with Your Nervous System 81

Chapter 9: You Can Heal Your Brain by Changing
Your Mindset 93

Chapter 10: Meditation Makes a Difference 106

Chapter 11: Just Breathe 121
Chapter 12: Get Your Body on Board 135
Chapter 13: Treatment Modalities to Help You Heal.........149
Chapter 14: Life Changes for Sustained Healing...............168

Resources 181
Endnotes...183
Acknowledgments 189
About the Author...191

Introduction

***

Remember...you can't begin the next chapter of your amazing life when you keep repeating the last one.

***

Whether you realize it or not, every day you are living the story of your life.

Imagine you are holding a large book in your hands. There is a golden bookmark in the center of the book. You put your fingers on the bookmark and open to that page. As your gaze rests on this place, you discover it is completely blank—a fresh new page, and it represents where you are today.

You then flip back in the book to the pages before the bookmark. They are filled up with all the events and circumstances from your birth until now. Everything that has happened in your life up to today is part of your story. It is already written.

You can't go back and change this part of your story—even if you want to. But you can learn from it and use the lessons to create the next chapter of your life with more intention.

Herein lies the problem that many entrepreneurs and business leaders face today. A significant challenge or trauma you have faced can lie dormant and unresolved for years, even decades, and can keep you from your ultimate potential.

No matter how many positive experiences you have had in your life, there is often a nagging issue from the past that holds you back from true freedom to live the life of joy and significance that you desire.

And here is the interesting part—you may not even fully comprehend it. I was certainly in that place for many years.

You see, I did a superior job of looking like I had it all together on the outside—as the kind yet kick-ass boss, the inspiring leader, the award-winning entrepreneur, the woman with a perfect family—but inside was a very different story.

Inside, I had shut away trauma that was so painful and so deep I didn't know it was there.

Until one day on a flight home from California.

It had been a fun and relaxing weekend getaway with a dear girlfriend and fellow entrepreneur. Living in different parts of the country, we didn't get to see each other a lot other than our business meetings in various cities a few times a year. That made this in-person time, just the two of us, even more special. We had stayed in a gorgeous hotel on the Pacific Ocean and enjoyed a perfect couple of days of beachside walks, decadent food, and deep conversations. Sunday came around far too quickly, and it was time to say goodbye.

The first leg of my flight was uneventful and had a layover in Seattle, Washington. All that was left was a quick thirty-minute flight home from Seattle to Bellingham. It was dark outside by the time our flight began to board. I remember walking onto the small plane and finding out that my seat had been changed at the last minute. I was seated in a window seat toward the back of the plane. As we waited on the tarmac the captain came on the overhead speakers letting us know the flight would be bumpy due to a storm in the area. Though I didn't like the thought of experiencing any turbulence, I told myself, "It's just a short flight. Then you will be home."

Within minutes of takeoff the plane was whipped by the wind. The captain came on, reminded everyone to stay in their seats with their seatbelts fastened, and asked the flight attendants to stay seated for the duration of the flight. I could feel the anxiety building in my chest as the farther we flew toward Bellingham, the rougher the turbulence became.

At one point, the small plane dropped heavily, and you could hear audible gasps from other passengers. Looking around in the darkness, my fear escalated, my heart raced, and I gripped the sides of my seat. Meanwhile, the woman next to me, who just happened to be a flight attendant heading home, was calm as could be. She gazed at me and without saying a word reached up over my head to turn the fan on my face. I remember thinking simultaneously to myself, *That was nice of her* and *Who would ever do this for a living?*

After twenty minutes (that felt like hours), the captain reported it was time to descend. My anxiety lessened briefly as I knew we would soon be landing. Unfortunately, the ride only got rougher, and the plane pitched and weaved. After several attempts, the captain announced, "I am sorry folks, we are being asked to turn around for your safety. We are heading back to Seattle."

When we finally landed and I got off the plane, my entire body shook in an episode of indescribable fear. I began to sob uncontrollably. Standing in the middle of the airport with people milling around me, I found I couldn't stop—it was like the floodgates had opened, and pent-up emotions of many years poured out of me.

Looking around, I noticed everyone else that had gotten off the flight with me appeared fine, and I definitely was not okay. Something was very wrong.

I thought, *How am I going to get home? There is no way I am getting back on a plane.* Through my tears, I called my husband to let him know he would simply have to come and get me. He was willing to make the two-hour drive. Then my daughter came on the phone and attempted to calm me down and convince me to wait it out and take another flight home. I recognized in her voice the gentle tone I used with her when she was upset as a child.

With my daughter's encouragement and the help of a kind agent, I finally calmed down and eventually got another flight safely home that evening. But the overreaction and high charged emotions I displayed were puzzling. I didn't understand them at first.

What had happened? What I would realize later was this: The trauma that I had buried for so long was making its debut. It not only had risen to the surface—it was boiling over. Whether I wanted to or not, it was time to deal with it.

As I sought and received help, I learned how common my situation was. That countless successful entrepreneurs and business leaders today, though their outer world appears picture-perfect, have an inner world of pain that has not been fully addressed…or addressed at all. And it's holding them back from being all that they are called to be.

So, let me ask you this: *Is it possible that you are missing out on your best life because of the pain of your past?*

You may think, as I did, that everything is going alright, better than alright, in fact. But at times, maybe in the dark hours of the night, do you sometimes wonder? If something really fell off the rails, how would you handle it? Do you recognize there is something holding you back from living up to your full potential?

> Is it possible that you are missing out on your best life because of the pain of your past?

I've been there. I know how you feel. I had everything going for me, until I didn't. It took me years to uncover the problem and create true freedom and peace in all areas of my life.

This book shares my journey out of the trauma that had held me captive for over thirty years. I wrote *Your Way Back to Happy* as personal testament of one's ability to truly heal your body and mind and begin anew. But more importantly, I want to share these learnings and the path that I took with other entrepreneurs who have fought a similar battle.

My friend, no matter what you have been through, I want you to know, without a shadow of a doubt, that you can take back control of your life. There is hope, even when you may feel like there is none. There is a way back to the happiness, inner peace, and confidence you once knew. Imagine stepping up your leadership to a whole new level, operating from a deeper, richer, more authentic space. It's time to uncover and free yourself completely from the challenges of your past and embrace endless possibilities for your future.

That's what we are going to do here together in this book. In Part One, you will gain a better understanding of the problem of unresolved trauma. You will learn how common it is for your past pain to hide, often within your entrepreneurial success. It can be frustrating to discover that the sheer grit and determination that have worked well in helping you to rise as a business leader won't work to heal your past pain. This knowledge can make you feel powerless. But don't worry. There is a way to reclaim your power—you just need the right tools. I am going to show you how step by step.

In Part Two, you will learn the practical applications needed to address and heal your past trauma. I will share the specific tools that I used to reclaim and radically change my life. You will get to know, on a deeper level, the workings of the beautiful body that is protecting you, and I will show you how to release what is no longer is serving you.

Most importantly, you will learn how to sustain this healing by making changes to how you are living your life on a day-to-day basis going forward. This will become your roadmap for building resilience and maintaining your healing for the rest of your life.

Are you ready? Let's get started.

PART ONE
Understanding the Problem

Chapter 1

You Look Fine, but You Are Not Fine

Your inner world is trying to get your attention. Are you listening?

There's nothing like a big decade birthday that makes you think more deeply about your life. As my fiftieth birthday drew closer, I began to think more about my health in the long term. Though I have always taken good care of myself—checking the box of the standard annual checkups, exercising regularly, and eating healthy most of the time—I wanted to kick it up a notch.

I read a health statistic that the average life expectancy of the late seventies was changing. Instead, in today's modern world, if you are relatively healthy at fifty years old, you will likely live to one hundred plus. I didn't care as much about the "living to one hundred" part as I did about "living every day healthy and active" for as long as possible.

Most of us would probably agree that the years of our life are not as important as the "life" in our years. Who doesn't want to stay active with high energy and be able to keep up with the great grandkids?

Since neither my husband nor I approach anything halfway, we went "all in" to learn as much as we could about improving our healthy lifestyle and longevity. This led me to the work of Dr. Daniel G. Amen, a physician and psychiatrist with a mission to revolutionize brain health and end mental illness in the process. After reading his compelling book *Change Your Brain, Change Your Life*, I had a whole new fascination with my brain.

One of the facts he pointed out was that the brain seems to be the only important organ in the body that we rarely test to see how healthy it is. Millions of people in the world today struggle with anxiety, depression, and various mental disorders. Yet, when someone seeks treatment for mental health issues, the doctor will frequently prescribe a medication based solely on the patient's reported symptoms and complaints, versus conducting specific tests on the brain. Think of this in terms of what we do for every other area of the body: if you go in for a symptomatic heart issue, the doctor will typically order an electrocardiogram or similar stress test.

There are countless stories of people experiencing mood issues, anxiety, or depression who were prescribed antidepressants or anti-anxiety medication when this may not have been the best course of treatment.

An example of this is Dr. Amen's own nephew: At nine years old, the child began acting out and attacked a little girl on the playground for no reason. Where most psychiatrists would likely have medicated the child, Dr. Amen took a brain scan first. The scan showed a golf ball sized cyst on his left temporal lobe, which was then removed surgically correcting the problem. No medication would have fixed this issue.

Think about it...your brain is a critical organ for your body to live and function, yet it is rarely evaluated when there are mental health concerns, and even more rarely as a preventative measure.

Why Settle for Just Good Health?

This made so much sense to Graham and me. We all want to have a healthy brain and a long healthy life; therefore, why wouldn't we take steps to ensure we are taking the absolute best care of it?

When we learned that many other medical professionals now approve of conducting brain scans to determine baseline brain health, we signed up for a SPECT (single photon emission computed tomography) scan for our next annual checkup, along with bloodwork and the other routine tests. Even though the scan wasn't covered by insurance, it was worth it to us to have a more complete picture of how our brains were functioning. We felt like it was another way to invest in our future together.

Some good friends of ours (another married couple) had the tests and confirmed how helpful they were. Not only did it provide them with a baseline on their brain health, but it also showed the differences in their brain type and how and why they communicate differently.

I was excited about the thought of having the SPECT scan and believed I could learn something about myself and how to take better care of my health for the future. I didn't know then what a revelation it would truly be.

My husband and I made the appointments which consisted of a total of three visits. First, we performed various tests to determine our brain type and executive functioning, then moved on to two scans of the brain where we had to lie still in a large machine that moved over us, similar to a regular CTO scan or MRI.

I remember feeling apprehensive walking into the test room. Admittedly the equipment is intimidating—the room's lighting was bright and in front of me was what looked like a large metal tube with essentially a table hanging out of it. "I can do this," I thought to myself. The technician was supportive as she strapped me in, then she slid me back into the tube for about twenty minutes each time. Though noisy, the procedure was uneventful, and before I knew it, the test was over.

The Results

Graham and I were excited for the follow-up appointment with the doctor, where we could learn what brain type we were, and what we could do to improve our function and performance. When we got to the clinic, Dr. Seyffert asked if we wanted to have the appointment together or separate.

"Together," we said in sync.

Graham went first. As a child, he had been diagnosed with ADHD, so we expected to learn more about this. We were amazed when the doctor showed us a small-yet-obvious indent in the brain where there was an old traumatic brain injury (TBI). He had an accident when he was three years old where he was hit in the head with a baseball bat by a neighbor boy.

The scan also clearly showed a brain with ADHD. Typically, people with ADHD tend to have a higher brain wave ratio of theta and beta compared to people without it. Dr. Seyffert showed both of us what a typical brain looks like of a healthy high functioning brain versus Graham's SPECT scan. It was fascinating to see these differences so clearly on the scan. He then talked with us about a treatment program for improvement.

Then it was my turn.

Dr. Seyffert turned to me and asked, "Do you know what PTSD is?"

"Sure," I said, a bit puzzled by the question. "Post-traumatic stress disorder." I then went on to say, "That's what people get after being through severe trauma. Like veterans of war."

He then referred to the SPECT scan of a healthy brain, pointing out the amygdala, located in the center of the midbrain and commonly called the fear center of the brain. I noticed this area appeared dark and peaceful. Next to the first scan, he then placed a second one showing the scan of a typical brain with PTSD. On this scan, the amygdala was lit up brightly. He told us that was because severe trauma puts someone in a constant fight-or-flight mode. The trauma has had such a profound impact that the brain is unable to let it go and continues to fire off warning signals.

"That makes sense," I said. "With someone in the war who has witnessed a horrific situation that is over and above anything they have experienced before, it is understandable it would have that effect on the brain."

With the PTSD scan on the table in front of us, he pulled out my scan and laid it down next to it. "Janelle, I wanted to show you this other scan to help you understand yours."

As I compared the two images side by side, I was surprised to see that my brain scan looked identical to the other scan with the amygdala lit up like NYC's Times Square.

He then dropped the bombshell. "Your scan shows a classic PTSD brain. It appears you have been through immense and ongoing trauma in your life. Janelle, you have PTSD."

For a moment I sat there stunned, finding it hard to believe what I was hearing. Within me, an inner conflict began. *This makes no sense—you have an amazing life. You have overcome your challenges*, one part of me said. Another part argued, *Wow, Janelle, this explains so much.*

Just a week after getting this report, I would have that airport meltdown that I described in the introduction. I believe there is important significance to this timing. Over the years, God was preparing me for this moment. You see, through his provision, he removed me from an unhealthy relationship many years before and guided me to rebuild my life into something beautiful. Now, after many years in the safe space of a husband who cherished me, I was ready to face the challenges of my past.

It May Be Your Time Too

How about you? If you take a moment and look at yourself in the mirror, how are you really doing?

There is a reason you picked up this book. Maybe you, like me, recognize you have been through some tough challenges, and think you have put them behind you. You work diligently to be the best version of yourself—you have a positive mindset, adopt the newest and best success habits, and eat healthy and exercise—yet something is still holding you back.

Or, you know you have unresolved trauma that continues to be activated despite doing everything else "right." If this is the case:

- You may have tried a number of things and they aren't working.
- You are tired of how powerless you sometimes feel.
- You remember a time you were really happy and want that again.
- You have a deep desire to take your power back and simply don't know how.
- You want to fully heal your mind and body.

> You work diligently to be the best version of yourself—you have a positive mindset, adopt the newest and best success habits, and eat healthy and exercise— yet something is still holding you back.

Though my leadership and life were in a good place the day I was diagnosed with PTSD, I didn't know how much better, richer, and happier I could be. But to get there was going to require a deep inner work.

Your inner world is trying to get your attention. Are you listening?

Chapter Reflection

Reflect on the events and circumstances of your life, and answer the following questions:

1. What is a significant challenging event or time of your life, and how has it shaped you?

2. What was the turning point that compelled you to address it?
3. Where has your inner world clashed with your outer world? This refers to what others see versus the reality of what's going on inside.
4. Do you sense that your inner world has been trying to get your attention? In what ways?

Reflection Exercise

Evaluate the following statements to see what best describes where you are today. Check as many boxes as applicable:

☐ You are proud of the challenges you have overcome in your life.

☐ You want to continue to grow in your leadership and day-to-day resilience.

☐ You find that despite your success, something is still holding you back from your full potential.

☐ You have tried a number of things to fix your physical and mental health and they aren't working—or work only for a while.

☐ You are tired of how powerless you sometimes feel.

☐ You remember a time you were really happy and want that again.

☐ You have a deep desire to take your power back and live from a place of deeper freedom, peace, and joy.

☐ You want to fully heal your mind and body.

Chapter 2

Your Trauma Doesn't
Need to Be Your Prison

———

*Trauma can often feel like an invisible prison, binding
you with chains you can't see but can deeply feel.*

———

The phone rang loudly next to me, waking me out of a deep,
early morning sleep. Half awake, I immediately started to
panic. As I groggily reached for my cell phone, I felt my heart
racing within me...

Then I saw the caller ID—it was just a spam call.

There was a reason for my reaction. Just a few weeks prior,
I had woken up to an emergency phone call that my dad had
been taken by ambulance to the hospital. Then the following
day, I was woken again by a call that my mother was in the
hospital too.

The summer of 2022 was a challenging time for our family
as my dear father began what became a one-year battle with

prostate cancer and a rollercoaster of events with hospital and doctor visits. Understandably, the surprises and constant uncertainty left me jittery. When I am truly honest with myself, the real battle is with fear.

Fear—that demon I now recognize who would love to hold you and I back from everything we are meant to be.

Sometimes, despite your best efforts, fear takes over. It is a familiar feeling for many of us, especially those who have been through significant trauma.

Trauma and its number one emotion of seemingly inescapable fear can leave you feeling powerless. It can often feel like an invisible prison, binding you with chains you can't see but can deeply feel. See if you recognize any of these common body sensations:

- The tightness in your chest feels like a vice-like grip on your heart.
- You have a pit in your stomach that won't go away.
- Sometimes it is so bad you feel like you are going to be sick.
- You have a hard time catching your breath.
- You feel a massive headache coming on.

But here's the good news: Fear and anxiety do not need to rule your life. You can learn how to let go of fear's grip. You can move from a mindset of fear to a mindset of freedom and peace. I have done it, and you can too.

The first step on this journey is understanding the root cause of these emotions—what trauma actually is and how it affects you.

The Heart of the Matter: What Trauma Really Is

Trauma is not merely an event that happened to you, but something that lives on inside you—deep within your nervous system, your mind, and your body. It's an imprint that, when left unresolved, can shape the way you perceive the world, the way you interact with others, and the way you lead in your business and personal life.

Each of us has had a traumatic experience at some point in our lives, regardless of whether it left us with an obvious case of post-traumatic stress.

Dr. Peter Levine, a renowned expert in the field of trauma and somatic experiencing, emphasizes the pervasive nature of trauma in his various research and work with clients over many decades. He found trauma has become so commonplace that most people don't even recognize its presence. It affects everyone.[1]

For entrepreneurs and business leaders, this lingering trauma can become a silent yet pervasive force. It's not just about the sleepless nights or the anxiety that hovers in the background—it's about how this unresolved pain can steer your decisions, cloud your judgment, and undermine your ability to lead effectively.

You may find yourself reacting to situations with an intensity that doesn't quite match the moment or feeling overwhelmed by tasks that you once handled with ease. This is your trauma speaking, your body and mind still caught in the grip of the past, unable to fully release and move forward.

To better understand trauma, it's essential to recognize its three main types: acute, chronic, and complex.

Acute Trauma—One Thing. This type of trauma results from a single, distressing event, such as an accident, natural disaster, or sudden loss. The intensity of the experience can overwhelm one's ability to cope, leading to a disruption in your sense of safety and stability.

Chronic Trauma—Ongoing. Unlike acute trauma, chronic trauma is the result of prolonged or repeated exposure to highly stressful events. This could include situations like ongoing abuse, persistent bullying, or living in a war zone. Chronic trauma wears down the nervous system over time, often leading to long-term emotional and psychological difficulties.

Complex Trauma—Many Things. This form of trauma typically involves exposure to multiple traumatic events, often of an invasive and interpersonal nature. Complex trauma is frequently seen if one has experienced childhood abuse, neglect, or domestic violence. It's often characterized by difficulties in relationships and self-regulation, as well as a deeply ingrained sense of shame or worthlessness.

Recognizing which type of trauma you're dealing with is the first step in reclaiming your power. Each type of trauma carries its own set of challenges but understanding them allows you to begin the process of healing and transformation.

But trauma isn't just about the events you've experienced; it's also about the pervasive emotions that linger long after the events have passed. Understanding these emotions is key to breaking free from their hold and stepping into a life of peace and purpose.

Let's become famil-iar with several difficult emotions prevalent in those who have suffered traumatic situations.

Twelve Pervasive Emotions of Trauma

Many of us, whether we realize it or not, carry the weight of our past with us. Traumatic experiences, big or small, can leave emotional fingerprints on our minds and hearts.

> Recognizing which type of trauma you're dealing with is the first step in reclaiming your power. Each type of trauma carries its own set of challenges but understanding them allows you to begin the process of healing and transformation.

These emotions can affect our leadership, our relationships, and our day-to-day decisions. Recognizing them is the first step in the healing journey.

To fully understand how trauma is impacting you, it's important to become aware of these emotions that persistently affect you. Here are examples of twelve pervasive emotions often associated with a traumatic past:

1. **Fear.** At the core of trauma is fear, which is an over-whelming feeling of dread or apprehension, often caus-ing hypervigilance, or a constant state of alert.

   This isn't your run-of-the-mill nervousness before a big presentation; it's a deep-rooted dread. You may experience this as having a pit in your stomach that comes on without any seeming reason or excessive worry and ruminating thoughts about a situation.

The way fear manifests and influences actions can vary greatly from one person to another. It can lead to seemingly contradictory behaviors, such as becoming overly cautious, limiting the risks you take in business and in life, or, conversely, taking excessive risks.

2. **Shame.** This is a deep feeling of guilt, incompetence, or unworthiness, even if the traumatic event was not your fault.

Shame can make you feel unworthy, like you're perpetually in the wrong. It's that nagging voice that says you're not enough, that you're an imposter in your own life.

In leadership, this can cause you to second guess yourself, ultimately preventing you from stepping into your power and making authoritative decisions.

3. **Sadness.** In the context of trauma, sadness isn't just a fleeting emotion; it can be a deep, pervasive feeling that colors your outlook on life, work, and relationships. While everyone feels down now and then, trauma-related sadness can be paralyzing, making even simple tasks feel monumental.

It can stem from a sense of loss—not just loss in the traditional sense, such as the death of a loved one, but also the loss of safety, control, or normalcy that trauma often brings.

Entrepreneurs, who are typically seen as strong, driven, and resilient, might find this emotion particularly conflicting, feeling pressured to maintain a facade of strength, even when they are struggling internally.

4. **Anger.** Whether it's directed inward or outward, anger is a potent emotion stemming from trauma. This could

be directed towards yourself, others, or the world in general, especially if you feel that an injustice has occurred.

It can be useful when channeled into passion for change, but destructive when it drives impulsive decisions or strains team dynamics.

5. **Guilt.** Close to shame, but distinct, guilt makes you feel responsible for events, even when they were out of your control.

I remember a time where it seemed I always felt guilty. When at work, I felt guilty that I wasn't with my kids like the other moms who got to stay at home... however, then when I was actually off work and with my kids, I felt guilty I wasn't at work and that in some way I was letting my team down.

6. **Hypervigilance.** This is a heightened state of sensory sensitivity accompanied by an exaggerated intensity of behaviors whose purpose it is to detect threats. If you have experienced severe trauma, this can manifest in various ways both psychologically and physically.

When I first heard this description, it felt like a bullseye, and I thought, *Wow, that is me.* Hypervigilance can make you feel constantly on edge, expecting or needing to protect yourself from potential threats. This can lead to an inability to relax or engage fully in activities. Physically this condition increases heart rate and a heightened startle response. For entrepreneurs, this can translate into an inability to delegate, trust, or let go of control.

Always being on high alert might have been a survival mechanism in the past, but it's exhausting in the long run.

7. **Betrayal.** A potent emotion that occurs when you have been let down by those you trust.

   When plagued by betrayal, you can develop deep-seated trust issues. For an entrepreneur facing this emotion, you may find it difficult to rely on partners, employees, or advisors.

   This lack of trust can lead to micromanagement as you may feel the need to oversee every detail personally in order to prevent potential betrayals.

8. **Confusion.** This occurs when you have difficulty making sense of your feelings or the event itself, leading to persistent rumination or denial.

   Trauma can skew your sense of reality. This confusion can lead to indecision and a lack of clarity in your entrepreneurial journey.

9. **Disconnection.** Sometimes, in the wake of trauma, you numb out. Disconnection is an emotional "shutting down," or feeling distant from your own emotions, experiences, or surroundings, often as a protective measure.

   You may feel disconnected from others, your work, and even yourself. For business leaders, this disconnection can lead to a sense of isolation, even when surrounded by a team.

10. **Loneliness.** This feeling of being isolated from others is often because you believe that no one can understand or relate to your experience.

    I remember the dark days of my own trauma after my husband abandoned our family and the intense feelings of loneliness. Even though I had dear friends and family who supported me, there seemed to be no escaping the "aloneness" I faced as a single mom.

11. **Hopelessness.** Perhaps one of the most challenging emotions, hopelessness can feel like a dark tunnel without an end. When you have endured significant trauma, especially that of a chronic nature, there will undoubtedly be days, weeks, or months where it feels like there is no end to the pain and change feels impossible.

    In business, this can manifest as a lack of vision or motivation for the future.

12. **Overwhelm.** Feeling overwhelmed is a common and formidable emotion for business leaders who have navigated the turbulent waters of past trauma. It's a state where the demands of leadership and the echoes of trauma converge, creating a storm of relentless pressure.

    The weight of these emotions can collectively lead to a sense that everything is just too much to handle. This state of being overwhelmed isn't just about the volume of work or the challenges of entrepreneurship; it's deepened by the unresolved emotional turbulence from past experiences. As a leader you may find that even routine decisions feel monumental, and the responsibility of guiding your team becomes a source of intense stress.

Remember, everyone's experience with trauma is unique, and not everyone will experience all or even any of these emotions in the same way.

The Way Out

Recognizing these emotions in yourself is the first step to understanding the prison you are trapped in. The next is understanding that these emotions, while valid and real, don't have to define your life or entrepreneurial journey.

You can acknowledge them, learn from them, and work through them. Remember, it's not about "moving on" but about "moving through."

As a leader, you have a unique platform and an opportunity. By addressing and healing your own trauma, you can pave the way for others, fostering understanding, empathy, and resilience in your team and community.

Take a moment today to reflect. Which of these emotions resonate with you? Understanding is the first step. From here, with support and commitment, healing and growth are not just possible; they're probable.

In the words of Steve Maraboli, "The truth is, unless you let go, unless you forgive yourself, unless you forgive the situation, unless you realize that the situation is over, you cannot move forward."

My friend, these emotions can cause you to feel bound and isolated, and I want you to know that I was there too, feeling that same way—it seemed like there was no one who really understood. In this next chapter, you will discover just how common it is for entrepreneurs to face unresolved trauma.

Chapter Reflection

As we conclude this chapter, I invite you to take a moment to reflect on the concepts we've explored. Healing begins with awareness, and this exercise is designed to help you identify the types of trauma that may be influencing your life and the emotions that accompany them.

Step 1. Reflect on the Three Types of Trauma

Acute Trauma. Recall any significant, singular events in your life that may have caused you distress. This could be a sudden loss, a severe accident, or an intense moment of fear or helplessness. Write down any such events that come to mind.

Chronic Trauma. Think about the situations or environments where you've experienced ongoing stress or emotional pain. This might include financial struggles, toxic relationships, or persistent challenges in your entrepreneurial journey. List these experiences.

Complex Trauma. Consider any patterns of emotional pain, particularly those rooted in relationships or long-term circumstances, that have affected your sense of self-worth and your interactions with others. Note any recurring themes or experiences.

Step 2. Name Your Trauma

Now that you've reflected on the different types of trauma, take a few minutes to write down how each of these traumas has manifested in your life. Naming your trauma is a powerful step in the healing process. It allows you to acknowledge what you've been through and begin to reclaim your power over it.

Step 3. Identify the Pervasive Emotions

Throughout this chapter, we've discussed the pervasive emotions that often accompany trauma—fear, anxiety, shame, helplessness, and more. Which of these emotions resonate most with you? Write down the emotions that you find yourself struggling with the most and consider how they might be connected to the trauma you've experienced.

Step 4. Personal Reflection

Take a few minutes to reflect on the connections between your identified traumas and the emotions you've listed. How have these experiences and feelings influenced your life, your decisions, and your business? Acknowledging these connections is the first step toward healing and transforming your life and entrepreneurial journey.

Step 5. Set an Intention for Healing

Finally, set a personal intention for healing. What do you want to achieve as you move forward on this journey? Whether it's finding peace, breaking free from fear, or embracing your true potential, write down your intention and keep it in mind as you continue through this book and your path to growth and healing.

Chapter 3

You Are Not Alone

---

*When you begin to take the steps needed to explore
your trauma, you may mistakenly believe you're the
only one who is silently battling past demons.*

It was June of 2022, and I sat amid 150 other business leaders
in Vancouver, British Columbia. As I gazed around the room the
atmosphere was charged, and it felt surreal to be looking at others'
faces—"Look Mom, no masks!" After all, it was the first time since
the pandemic two years before that the Canadian Association of
Professional Speakers had been together in person.

Admittedly, I was feeling a bit giddy. It seems strange now
to look back and remember how excited my husband and business partner, Graham, and I were to put on work clothes and
dress shoes. Everyone in the room was dressed up and looking
polished; you could hear squeals and laughter as members
who obviously hadn't seen each other in a while embraced.

I remember thinking to myself, "Wow, these are happy, successful people. They don't seem to be affected at all by what's happened."

Then the main keynote speaker stepped on stage—a renowned Hall of Fame recipient with an extremely successful career. I was looking forward to gleaning wisdom from this inspirational woman. I certainly got what I was hoping for but not in the way you think…

When she stepped on the stage she took in the room, gazing at all the eager faces with a warm smile on her face. Then she stated, "Take a look around the room at all of these successful people gathered together." The group did as she instructed. Then she said, "But let me tell you something. There is not *one* person in this room who has it all together, including me."

She went on to share with us how she struggled with her own mental health and had many bouts of significant depression. She recounted as the world of speaking shut down in the pandemic, she did personally as well, struggling some days to even get out of bed.

In a brave, "mic drop" moment this renown business leader had our attention. And she is not alone.

As we discussed in Chapter 1, in many cases you may look fine on the outside; however, the inside is a different story. When you begin to take the steps needed to explore your trauma, you may mistakenly believe you're the only one who is silently battling past demons. Rest assured, this is

> When you begin to take the steps needed to explore your trauma, you may mistakenly believe you're the only one who is silently battling past demons.

a common assumption, and you are definitely not the only one wrestling with this problem.

Trauma is More Common Than You May Think

Though many business leaders in that conference room and across the globe put on their game face every day to lead their business, often there are deep struggles hidden within. According to the World Health Organization (WHO), an astounding 70 percent of people in the world have suffered from trauma in their lifetime. The United States alone has seen a twofold increase in anxiety, depression, and hopelessness about the future since the pandemic, now classified as a major traumatic event.[2]

Unfortunately, as I am sure you have seen firsthand, society exacerbates this issue with a culture of bravado permeating the world of the entrepreneur and business leader. One is expected to and even *celebrated* when they have an exterior image that is picture-perfect.

At a recent conference, I had the privilege of taking a group of CEOs and leaders through my *Life Reset* keynote which included an interactive panel of a few of the top industry leaders. Prepping them in advance, I purposefully opened the door to ask about their own struggles as entrepreneurs, including mental health.

I believe that my willingness to start and share openly about my own struggles and path out of brokenness gave them permission to share their own experiences and defining moments. The audience was floored that each prestigious member of the panel shared they had faced or were facing a challenge with their mental health and well-being. Each one talked about hard professional and personal circumstances, burnout, and how for most of them it took a crisis to take their own well-being seriously.

Afterward, one of the audience members, a clinical psychologist, said she had never before sat in a room of successful business professionals and seen such vulnerability and transparency.

The Trend of Mental Health Issues and Awareness

The last decade has witnessed a significant rise in the awareness and diagnosis of mental health issues across various populations, including the realm of elite business leadership. This increase can be attributed to a combination of factors, including greater awareness and destigmatization of mental health, more accessible diagnostic tools, and the escalating pressures of modern professional environments.

Forgive me if I geek out on numbers for a moment here, but I think these insights and statistics on mental health trends are interesting and relevant to our conversation:

Increased Prevalence: According to the World Health Organization (WHO), depression and anxiety disorders cost the global economy approximately $1 trillion each year in lost productivity. This suggests a widespread impact that likely includes many within the upper echelons of business leadership.[3]

High-Pressure Environments: Elite business leaders often operate in high-stakes, high-stress environments that demand constant connectivity and availability. The relentless pace and pressure to perform can exacerbate or trigger mental health issues. A *Harvard Business Review* article highlighted that 50 percent of CEOs report experiencing feelings of loneliness, which can be a precursor to more severe mental health conditions.[4]

Entrepreneurial Stress: Entrepreneurs, in particular, are at risk, with studies indicating that more than 30 percent of startup founders report dealing with depression. No matter the strength and number of your team, "the buck stops" ultimately with you as the business owner and the weight is heavy on your shoulders not just while you are at work but around the clock. The uncertainties of business ventures combined with the isolation often experienced by leaders contribute to this heightened risk.[5]

Work-Life Imbalance: This is one of the top issues that I work on with my coaching clients. Unfortunately, it is harder today than it ever has been to separate work from home, as most business owners work remotely at least some if not all of the time. The digital era has blurred the lines between work and personal life, making disconnection increasingly difficult.

For business leaders, the expectation to be *perpetually on* leads to chronic stress, leaving you physically and emotionally exhausted, and eventually, if not dealt with, to burnout.

Everyone Has a White BMW

Though I have to say I am not car obsessed, nor frankly do I know a whole lot about the difference between horsepower and torque, I was pretty excited about my new BMW X5 being delivered from Dallas, Texas. It was white with a gorgeous leather interior and heated seats (how did ever survive without those?). I thought it was very unique and couldn't wait for it to arrive.

The funny thing is, after having the new car about a month, I came out of the store into the parking lot one day, walked over to my car, and couldn't unlock it. I then noticed the car was not mine—but one that looked just like it. Over the next few weeks, it seemed that everywhere I looked I saw another white BMW.

There is a common phenomenon called the "Baader-Meinhof phenomenon" or "frequency illusion." It occurs when something you've recently noticed, learned about, or thought about suddenly seems to appear with a surprising frequency in your daily life. This isn't because these things are actually appearing more often; rather, it's because you've become more attuned to noticing them.

Here's how it works:

Once your attention is captivated by something new or significant to you (like buying a new white BMW), your brain unconsciously keeps an eye out for it. This heightened state of awareness makes it more likely that you'll notice other white BMWs as you go about your day.

The Baader-Meinhof phenomenon is a type of cognitive bias. Our brains are wired to recognize patterns and make connections. When we encounter something new or significant, our brain tends to spot it more in our environment, creating a loop where we think it's suddenly more prevalent.

I only mention this as the same thing happened once I realized that I had unresolved trauma in my life. As I healed and began to speak openly about it, it seemed that every entrepreneur I spoke with also had faced deep challenges in their life, and many of them, not having fully dealt with it, or understood how their trauma was impacting their life and business.

Of course, this didn't mean that suddenly there was an increased number of entrepreneurs who had past trauma. This issue has always been there, and now that I was attuned to it in my own life, I was recognizing it in others.

How Your Trauma Manifests in Your Leadership

As you are undoubtedly beginning to see—you are not navigating the effects of past trauma alone. And, without you realizing, it is likely showing up in your leadership style as it does in mine. Don't worry—it's not all bad news.

In a lot of ways, those who have overcome immense challenges can become better leaders. You do need to understand how your trauma shows up in your leadership because—let's face it—you will navigate through your professional landscape with a blend of strengths and vulnerabilities, some of which are shaped by your past experiences. Trauma, an unwelcome visitor in anyone's life story, can leave an indelible mark on how you lead and engage with your team.

See if you recognize any of these traits in your own leadership:

- **Resilience and Grit**

    Got grit anyone? I can imagine you are saying a resounding "yes!" Trauma can foster an unparalleled resilience and grit in leaders, shaping you into an individual who can withstand and bounce back from setbacks more effectively.

This resilience is born out of necessity, as overcoming personal trauma often requires developing coping mechanisms and mental toughness.

If you are this type of leader, you will tend to approach business challenges with a problem-solving mindset, viewing obstacles as opportunities to learn and grow. Your past experiences teach you that difficulties can be surmounted, imbuing your leadership style with perseverance and a never-give-up attitude that can inspire and motivate your teams to tackle challenges head-on.

- **Empathy and Emotional Intelligence**

Leaders who have experienced trauma may develop a heightened sense of empathy and emotional intelligence, enabling you to connect with others on a deeper level.

Your own experiences with hardship can make you more attuned to the emotional states and needs of your employees, fostering a more supportive and understanding work environment.

This empathetic leadership style can lead to stronger, more cohesive teams, as employees feel seen, heard, and valued. However, the challenge lies in balancing empathy with the need to make tough decisions, ensuring that compassion does not cloud judgment.

(Are saying to yourself, "Yep, that's me"? My team used to lovingly call me the Queen of Third Chances.)

- **Innovative Problem-Solving**

Experiencing trauma can lead to innovative problem-solving skills in leadership. Difficult circumstances often make you have to think on your feet and develop creative solutions to navigate your personal challenges.

This adaptability can translate into a business context, where you may be someone that's more likely to think outside the box and encourage innovation within your teams.

You may not be afraid to take calculated risks or venture into uncharted territory if it means finding a solution to a pressing problem. However, the pendulum can swing in the opposite direction as well—sometimes the fear of failure or disappointment from the past may cause you to hesitate or procrastinate on dealing with problems, hoping they will magically go away.

- **Driven by a Strong Sense of Purpose**

  Leaders who have overcome trauma often emerge with a strong sense of purpose and a desire to make a meaningful impact. Your personal struggles can foster a deep sense of mission, driving you to pursue your business goals with passion and determination.

  This purpose-driven leadership can be incredibly motivating for employees, aligning your team around a common goal and fostering a sense of unity and dedication. In my own life, this contributed to me becoming a leader that others wanted to follow - growing my own team to several hundred members.

- **Overworking and Burnout**

  The drive to overcome and succeed can sometimes lead you to overwork yourself, setting an unsustainable pace that risks burnout. Your determination to prove yourself and achieve your goals can blur the boundaries between work and personal life, leading to exhaustion and decreased effectiveness over time.

In Part Two, I will be teaching you about the importance of self-care and strategies for setting healthy work-life boundaries. These tools are essential for you to maintain your well-being and continue leading effectively.

- **Trust Issues**

   Trauma can lead to trust issues, where you may find it challenging to delegate tasks or rely on others, fearing that your standards won't be met or that you will be let down.

   While being hands-on can ensure quality and accountability, it can also stifle team autonomy and innovation. Building trust is a key component for effective leadership, and your own trust issues can sometimes get in the way of this. In a later chapter, I will share some tools to foster a collaborative and dynamic work environment where everyone feels empowered to contribute their best.

- **Communication Challenges**

   A leader with a traumatic past may sometimes struggle with communication, either by being overly guarded about your thoughts and feelings or by being overly direct, as a defense mechanism.

   As I am sure you already know, effective communication is a cornerstone of successful leadership, so it's crucial for you to recognize your limitations in this area and to learn how to develop clear, open, and constructive communication skills. This includes learning to listen actively, express thoughts empathetically, and provide feedback in a way that supports growth and development.

- **Risk of Projecting Personal Issues**

There's a risk you may project your unresolved trauma onto your business practices and relationships, interpreting challenges through the lens of your past experiences rather than seeing them objectively.

One of my clients faced this problem when it came time to terminate someone on his team. A past situation where he had been betrayed by another long-term employee clouded his judgment. He was paralyzed to make a decision because he was seeing his current dilemma through the lens of the past.

As you can see, it is a complex issue, and the threads of past traumas will weave into your leadership style in both empowering and challenging ways.

It is exciting and refreshing to see successful leaders opening up and sharing their stories at our Success Life events. If you and I, and other entrepreneurs, can show that it is "okay to not be okay" and lead from a place of transparency and compassion, there will be a domino effect.

> If you and I, and other entrepreneurs, can show that it is "okay to not be okay" and lead from a place of transparency and compassion, there will be a domino effect.

Today as I write this, I am grateful there is growing support for accepting and addressing the mental health issues prevalent in today's world. But there is a long way to go. As business owners and managers, we simply must do a better job being trauma informed as we lead our companies, and it starts first by looking in the mirror.

Chapter Reflection

We discussed in this chapter a number of ways that trauma can impact your leadership style. Let's take a look at the eight different traits listed and see which ones resonate with you. For each of these below, answer whether this is a trait you have seen in yourself or others have seen in you, and what influence it has had. Where has it helped you? Where has it hurt you?

Leadership Trait

How have these traits shown up in your leadership?

- Resilience and Grit
- Empathy and Emotional Intelligence
- Innovative Problem-Solving
- Driven by a Strong Sense of Purpose
- Overworking and Burnout
- Trust Issues
- Communication Challenges
- Projecting Personal Issues

Chapter 4

From Pushing Through to Letting Go

———

*Perhaps the traits that made you a
successful entrepreneur are the very things
holding you back from your healing.*

———

In my journey to heal my own trauma, I went down several
roads and tried many different modalities to truly take my life
to another level. You will learn about all of these and more in
the second part of this book. But before we get there, allow me
to share a hard learning that took me far too long to grasp, and
I hope can save you some time.

The "lightbulb moment" came when I was learning about
neurofeedback, one of these healing methods that became transforming for me. If you aren't familiar with it, neurofeedback is a
brain training method that improves the function of your brain by
recording your brain activity in real time while you do a variety

of exercises. With practice, you can improve your brain's performance in focus and attention, along with healing areas of the brain affected by stress and trauma.

In one of these sessions with my psychologist Dr. Nathan Brown, I found myself increasingly frustrated by my inability to calm my mind during a meditation training session. Afterward, we reviewed the program together and I could see for myself the data showing what my brain was doing during the meditation session. *Instead of my brain calming as it should, it was revving up.*

Then Dr. Brown shared these wise words with me:

> "Janelle, there are times where your natural tendency to push through is not helpful."

His statement took me completely aback. "Wait," I answered. "This is how I have always succeeded."

What the Typical Entrepreneur Looks Like

In the entrepreneurial world, your ambition, relentless drive, and uncanny ability to turn challenges into opportunities are what set you apart. This spirit propels you forward, helping you to innovate, lead, and achieve the seemingly impossible.

Yet, there comes a moment in your journey, as my trained friend helped me realize, that this very drive, while leading to incredible business success, might not always serve you well on a personal level, especially when it comes to healing from past traumas.

After my airport meltdown and figuring out I had some serious unresolved trauma, I took the stance of the typical driven entrepreneur—you know the one:

- You're faced with a hurdle and dive deep into problem-solving mode.
- You gather all of the intel and strategize how to solve it.
- Through sheer hard work, discipline, and "giving it all you've got," you tackle it head on!

This approach is commendable in your business, but when it comes to the delicate work of healing, this 'fix it' mentality will fall short. And with this revelation comes the understanding that perhaps the traits that made you a successful entrepreneur—your efficiency, your tendency to push through—*are the very things holding you back* from healing.

> Perhaps the traits that made you a successful entrepreneur—your efficiency, your tendency to push through—*are the very things holding you back* from healing.

The Driven Personality

As a successful leader, your drive and ambition are not just tools for success but are deeply ingrained aspects of your personality. If you've taken any personality assessments you've likely found yourself landing in the "Achiever" category.

According to insights from the Birkman Method, a comprehensive favorite we use with our coaching clients, your goal-oriented nature and strategic vision are your strengths. However, when it comes to healing from unresolved trauma, these same traits can present unique challenges. See if you resonate with any of these achiever patterns:

Goal-Oriented Approach to Healing. Your instinct to set goals and aggressively pursue them is beneficial in many areas of life. However, healing from trauma doesn't adhere to the typical roadmap of achievement. It's not a peak to be conquered but a process to be experienced. The nonlinear nature of healing can be frustrating if you expect quick, clear results.

Critical Self-Evaluation. You hold yourself to exceptionally high standards, which can be a double-edged sword in trauma recovery. While striving for excellence can motivate you, it can also lead to self-criticism when progress in healing doesn't meet your expectations. This critical stance may hinder the acceptance and compassion necessary for true healing.

Strategic and Big-Picture Thinking. While your ability to see the big picture aids in business and leadership, it might make you overlook the small, gradual steps that are crucial in the healing process. Healing requires embracing the nuances and often the mundane aspects of daily self-care, which might not immediately align with strategic outcomes.

Independence. Your self-reliance is admirable and often necessary in entrepreneurial ventures, but in the realm of trauma recovery, this independence can become isolating. Healing often requires vulnerability and the ability to lean on others for support, whether it's therapists, support groups, or trusted friends. Learning to accept help is not a sign of weakness but a crucial step in the healing process.

Discomfort with Vulnerability. As someone who is used to being in control and leading others, facing your own vulnerabilities can be particularly challenging. Healing from trauma involves confronting painful memories and emotions, which can feel counterintuitive to your usual mode of maintaining strength and composure. Embracing vulnerability is essential for deep emotional healing.

Resisting the Slow Pace of Healing. The fast-paced, results-driven approach that defines your professional life can make the often slow and unpredictable pace of trauma healing seem frustrating. It's important to recognize that healing cannot be rushed and requires patience and persistence—qualities that might feel as foreign to you as they did to me but are essential for personal growth.

Understanding and acknowledging these aspects of your personality can empower you to approach your healing journey with a new perspective. It's not about changing who you are but about adapting your strengths in ways that also support your emotional and psychological well-being. Let's talk about why a different approach is important.

Why You Need a Different Approach to Heal Your Trauma

There is a balance that high achieving entrepreneurs (including myself) often miss. The balance between:

- Work and Rest
- Striving and Abiding
- Pressing On and Letting Go

As much as you may want to make healing your trauma *a goal to achieve*, the more you do this, the more elusive it will become.

> Healing requires a different kind of strength. It's not about pushing through; it's about letting go, about being present, and about allowing yourself to feel and process emotions you've long buried in the name of efficiency. This isn't a problem that can be 'solved' in the traditional sense—it's a journey that needs to be experienced, with all its ebbs and flows.

To my fellow driven entrepreneur who resonates with this narrative, know this: Your ability to overcome and adapt, to rise from challenges, doesn't just make you an exceptional business leader; it also equips you with the resilience needed for personal healing.

How You Go From Pushing Through to Letting Go

My friend, you have everything within you to heal your mind, body, and soul. But it requires a shift—a pivot from constantly pushing to gently allowing, from always doing to sometimes just being.

This lesson was a transformational change for me that finally began my healing—but it took unlearning pretty much everything I used to do to approach problems prior to my discovery.

Part of it was learning, as I shared in the last chapter, that the trauma I had lived with for most of my adult life impacted my leadership style in good and bad ways. Though there were positive traits that came out of my trauma I had to unlearn the negative ones, or, in this case, the ones that didn't work for my self-healing.

I needed to experience the complete opposite of effort, which was being in the present moment, or, in other words, being mindful.

> Though there were positive traits that came out of my trauma I had to unlearn the negative ones, or, in this case, the ones that didn't work for my self-healing.

What is Mindfulness?

Mindfulness is a state of awareness that comes from paying attention, on purpose, to the present moment.

Merriam-Webster defines it this way:

Mindfulness

1. *The quality or state of being mindful.*
2. *The practice of maintaining a nonjudgmental state of heightened or complete awareness of one's thoughts, emotions, or experiences on a moment-to-moment basis.*

also: *such a state of awareness*

Rather than effort, being present and mindful is about learning to let go and just "be." *Be* in the present moment—don't stew in regret over something in the past or worry over something in the future.

This is not easy to do in this fast-paced, heavily scheduled, you can do-it-all world. It is challenging to be mindful when your life is packed to the brim, and you are thinking of the next place you need to be.

Not only is there the societal pressure to have your own calendar packed, now if your kids don't have schedules as full as yours—with elite sports teams that go year around and personal trainers to make sure they don't fall behind their classmates, they are somehow missing out too.

I recall a time when my daughter and I were in the car together driving home from an evening concert at school. With college just a couple of short years away, we were having a conversation about her plans after high school. She had some ideas about what she wanted to do, but it didn't take long for the conversation to stress her out.

She suddenly looked over at me in exasperation and said, "Mom, can't we ever just live in the moment?"

Ouch...she made a good point. (*So much so I remember the conversation vividly to this day, several years later.*) It seemed then, with college pressure high and making those decisions paramount, that it was *all* we talked about.

As a parent, you want to ensure your kids are on the right path, and discussing future dreams and plans with them is important. However, if you have a constant emphasis on the future (or the past), you can miss out on being fully present in your life, your kid's lives, and the amazing gifts of "today."

Many in my entrepreneurial community have shared that being present is a top challenge.

See if this behavior sounds familiar:

- When you are with others, your mind often wanders to something else rather than being present and engaged.
- When by yourself, you spend so much time thinking about what you didn't get done yesterday or what you need to do tomorrow, you miss today.

- When you do have a free mental moment, your tendency is to grab your phone and start scrolling to fill any gaps in time.

I get it—it is hard to "just be," and I fight the same pull toward mental time travel, technology, or other distractions. But you can change your typical pattern and learn how to be truly present.

As we delve deeper into various healing modalities in the second part of this book, building a new habit of mindfulness is an essential first step. By learning to be present with yourself, you enhance not only your life, but also your journey toward healing.

Five Ways to Practice Being Present

1. Understand What Being Present Means

When you're truly present, you have all of your attention in that moment. You feel totally focused on what's happening right now and connected with yourself and everything around you.

If you're with your children, your partner, or a business associate, your full attention is on them—you tune out any distractions and truly listen to what they are saying.

Meditation is a helpful technique to learn how to be more mindful and present. Using your breath as a guide can help ground you in the moment and get you out of your head. This has been such an important practice for my own healing and well-being I have dedicated a chapter to it in this book.

2. Reconnect with Nature

Being in nature is a wonderful way to be present, and crucial for your health and well-being. There are many health benefits of spending time in the great outdoors—including reduced risk of anxiety, depression, heart disease, and more.

Multiple studies have linked nature walks with improved mental health. Why wouldn't you want to do something that is known to lower your stress and brighten your mood?

Walk outside today—even if it's just around your neighborhood—and notice how much better you feel when you're immersed in nature (versus urban life). Be in the moment by breathing in the fresh air. Smell the fragrances, notice the colors of the sky and the landscape around you.

If you live in a city with little outdoor space, find a nearby park or trails to go on. Schedule vacations where you can get out and spend as much time as possible in nature—the ocean, the mountains, or the national forests.

3. Create Mental Boundaries

When you're overactive and too focused on details, it's easy to lose sight of your overall goals. By creating mental limits for yourself, you can refocus on what really matters—your healing and well-being.

For example, if your goal is to stop and think before acting, tell yourself you can only respond after counting down from five in your head or after taking three deep breaths.

If you tend to stretch your boundaries for the sake of others, it may be time to do a self-check. Understand your own limits and set boundaries that keep you grounded in what matters most.

4. Let Go of Distractions

Your life is full with countless responsibilities of work and home. As a high achiever, you may love it that way and not want to let any of it go. It just would be great if it were a little bit easier to manage it all.

With so much on your plate, there are many distractions. And sometimes it can feel like you need to be constantly connected and on call. But you have the power to disconnect from time to time, and it is critical to your well-being.

As a start, find some time every day where you can be alone away from distractions, to reconnect with yourself. Even if it's only for a few minutes a day. By letting go of distractions, you'll have time to slow down and tune into your inner thoughts.

5. Focus on What's Right in Front of You

In today's world, your life is constantly overstimulated. And when it comes to being more present with yourself, it can be tempting to turn off that overstimulation by tuning out—as in checking out mentally.

The problem is that in tuning out, you miss things that are important to you—happening right now. The best way to practice being present is to focus on what is right in front of you: your partner, your kids, whatever you're doing at work or school.

Tune into conversations and events as they happen; live them rather than watch them pass by like a movie on repeat. With attention, you can catch yourself when you zone out, and tune in to the people you love and the events you want to remember. This practice helps you stay grounded, which is especially critical for those of us on a healing path.

Practice Being Mindful Throughout the Day

You may start your day feeling present and centered, but then find you get stressed and scattered as the day goes on.

How many times do you start with a quiet time in the morning, but then find yourself in the frenzy of regular activity that comes with the responsibilities of day-to-day life? Your mind begins to race—rather than being present, you find yourself thinking about the next thing on your to-do list.

When the world these days is one of frenetic activity and high stress, it takes real intention to not live your life that way.

But you have a choice here, my friend. You can choose to say no to a frenetic pace that erases your ability to be present. You can also choose to not get caught up in the frenzy of others—

- It's their frenzy and doesn't have to be yours.
- It's their attitude and doesn't need to become yours.
- It's their bad day and doesn't need to become yours.

There are a number of ways you can practice being mindful throughout the day. The main objective is to "be" wherever you are. This means that you focus only on the task at hand, keeping distractions at bay.

Here are a few mindful ideas for you to consider:

- **During a Shower.** When you take a shower, just take a shower. Don't think of what you have to do next or plan out your day. Instead, enjoy the warmth of the water running over you and give yourself a little massage as you soap over your neck and shoulders.
- **On Phone Calls.** When you are on a phone call, be on the phone call. Close out your email or task at hand

and decide to be present and engaged with the person you care about on the other end.

- **In Physical Activities.** Be at your yoga or exercise class. Focus on your breath or the specific moves you are doing. When your mind wanders, simply bring it back.
- **At the Dinner Table.** Be present with your family at the dinner table. Savor the tantalizing smells and taste of your food and enjoy the interactions with your family members.
- **While Watching a Sunset.** Move away from your devices and get outside. Simply sit and enjoy the last rays of the day. This soothes the mind and also reconnects you with the simple joys of life.

By embracing these practices, you're not just healing your body from trauma; you're enriching your life with deeper connections and a renewed appreciation for the present. This approach helps shift the focus from a purely goal-driven recovery to a more balanced, sustainable path of healing and personal growth.

Every mindful moment you cultivate is a step toward reclaiming control over your life—a journey we will explore in greater depth in the next chapter. There, we'll uncover practical strategies to empower you to break free from the confines of trauma and embrace a life of freedom and choice.

Chapter Reflection—Problem-Holding vs. Problem-Releasing Exercise

Objective: This exercise aims to help you recognize the difference between holding onto a problem tightly (pushing through) and releasing it (letting go), and to experience how each approach affects your stress levels, creativity, and problem-solving abilities.

Materials Needed:

- A small, physical object to represent your problem (e.g., a stone or a small toy)
- A journal and pen

Instructions:

1. **Identify a Current Problem:** Think of a current challenge or problem in your business or personal life that you've been trying to solve by pushing through.
2. **Physical Representation:** Hold the object you've chosen to represent this problem in your hand. Grip it tightly, symbolizing how you've been holding onto the problem. Notice the tension in your hand and arm.
3. **Reflect and Write:** While gripping the object, reflect on the following questions. Write your answers in your journal:
   - How does holding onto the problem this tightly make you feel physically? Emotionally?
   - In what ways have you been pushing through to solve this problem? List specific actions and strategies.
   - What has been the result of this approach so far?
4. **Releasing the Object:** Now, slowly open your hand, and release the object onto a soft surface. Observe the sensation of letting go.
5. **Reflect and Write Again:** With your hand now open and relaxed, reflect on the following questions. Write your responses:

- How does the act of releasing the object make you feel in contrast to holding it tightly?
- Can you envision a way to approach your problem with a mindset of letting go rather than pushing through? What might that look like?
- Identify one small step you can take today that embodies this approach of letting go.

6. **Commitment:** Choose the one step you identified and commit to taking it within the next twenty-four hours. Note it as a commitment in your notebook.

7. **Follow-Up:** After taking the step, reflect on the experience. Did approaching the problem with the intention of letting go change the outcome or your feelings about the situation?

Review:

- Reflect on the overall experience of this exercise.
- Consider how the physical act of holding and then releasing can metaphorically apply to problem-solving in your life.
- Think about how you might integrate a balance between pushing through and letting go in future challenges.

Chapter 5

You Have the Power to Take Back Control of Your Life

---

*"You've always had the power my dear,
you just had to learn it for yourself."
—Glinda, The Wizard of Oz*

You can have a great plan for your life, but sometimes it takes an unexpected turn. This happened to me.

It was the Monday of a typical work week, the fast-paced blur where you look at the clock and can't believe the workday is over already and you need to get home. I didn't know then it would become a pivotal day, one now forever engrained in my memory.

As founder of a growing facility management business, I had a number of meetings that day and had been out since the early morning. It had been a full but productive day, and I looked forward to getting home to my family.

Arriving at my house, I pulled into our driveway, shut off the car, grabbed my bag from the back seat, and headed into the house. Used to mayhem when I got home, the house seemed unusually quiet, but I didn't think much of it. Not seeing the kids or my husband, I went into the office and dropped off my work bag. I then saw my two youngest daughters through the office window playing out on the swings in the backyard. They were four and seven years old at the time.

I thought to myself, *That's strange, I wonder where their dad is?* I realized then my husband's truck wasn't in the yard, something I hadn't noticed when I first got home. Where could he be? The kids had been left in his care that day!

I walked out the office door and down our patio steps to the backyard and went over to my girls, Payton and Paige. As soon as they saw me, they ran up to me and threw their arms around me. After our usual hellos, I asked them, "Girls, where is your dad?" That's when Payton, my seven-year-old, somberly looked at me and said, "Daddy isn't here. He left with a suitcase."

My stomach dropped. What is going on? My kids had been left home alone for who knows how many hours. My husband was gone, without any notice, without any warning, and he intentionally abandoned his family.

This wasn't the first time he had dropped off the grid with his various cycles of addiction, but I knew in my heart there was finality to this time. Payton told me that he said he was going to go visit a friend, though when we went in the house, I found a small envelope on the counter with my name on it. In it was his own "Dear John" note to me stating he was not coming back and to not bother trying to contact him.

The stillness of the house matched my heart as I felt frozen in time. I became numb. I didn't want to face the reality that what I had dreaded for years had actually happened. It was so surreal. Just the night before, my husband and I had taken a walk together talking about the upcoming week, the kids' activities, and our plans for the next family vacation.

With mechanical precision, I moved through the familiar evening routine of making dinner, cleaning up, checking the next day's schedule, and getting the girls ready for bed.

> Looking back, I was in shock. I was doing everything I could do at the time—trying to keep things normal for the girls, even though inside I was frantic.

With baths done and teeth brushed, my daughters were in their matching fluffy robes—white with pink and blue bears. I can still smell the baby shampoo in their hair. How little they were, so precious—my everything. Then Paige, my four-year-old asked me, "Mommy, when is Daddy coming home?"

Looking at the concern in their eyes and the million questions bouncing around in their little heads, I simply knew I couldn't lie to them in the same way their father did.

I got down on my knees and took them in my arms to tell them the truth. "Girls, your daddy left, and I don't think he will be coming back."

This began the closing chapter of what had been a long and excruciating journey of eighteen years. My first husband didn't come back, and we eventually divorced. Living in the aftermath, the next several years were exceedingly difficult.

My oldest daughter was able to find her escape at college the next year and I was glad she had a new environment and path to focus on. Meanwhile, my two youngest battled every day. One was withdrawn and quiet, the other angry and extremely anxious.

Both struggled with deep grief and confusion, and there were many nights they cried themselves to sleep. I kept telling them we would be okay. I said to them, "Listen girls, I know this is hard, but in time we will feel better. Everything will be okay. We've got each other, and we will get through it together."

One day, I got a call at work from my daughter's pre-school. "We had a fire-drill practice," they said, "and it really scared Paige. She started shaking and crying during the drill, and we haven't been able to calm her down. Can you come and get her?"

"Of course," I said, "I will leave right now." I quickly drove to the school—about a twenty-minute drive away and found her still white as a ghost and shaking. I wrapped her in my arms, gritting my teeth and trying not to have my own meltdown in front of her teacher.

Later that afternoon when I got the kids home from school and had a few moments to myself, I remember walking into my bedroom and shutting my door. It was one of those days it felt impossible to go on, and more than anything, I wanted to crawl into a ball in the corner of my bedroom and never get up.

When Your Life is Out of Control

As we discussed in Chapter 2 your trauma can feel like a prison you just can't escape from. This was how I felt that day, and I am sure you can relate as you have struggled with your own challenges. Unresolved trauma can seem like an invisible chain, binding you in ways that profoundly impact your sense of control.

You Have Learned to Be Helpless

After my PTSD diagnosis, I was determined to learn everything I could about trauma. A therapist recommended the book *The Body Keeps the Score*, by Dr. Bessel van der Kolk. Although it reads like a textbook, it's well worth the effort—I gained a wealth of knowledge about trauma and its impacts.

I couldn't figure out why I didn't leave the unhealthy relationship I had been in for so many years. One of my girlfriends said to me, "We had no idea what you were going through. If it was that bad, why did you stay?" Described by my friends and family as "one of the strongest people they knew" they didn't understand, and frankly, neither did I. Then I read about a stunning study that became a lightbulb moment. (Note: this study is disturbing to read.)

In 1967, Martin Seligman and Steven Maier at the University of Pennsylvania conducted an experiment. The study involved a group of dogs that were placed in harnesses and subjected to electric shocks that they could not escape. Initially, the dogs would attempt to avoid the shocks by lurching away, but they quickly learned that their actions had no impact on stopping the shocks.

After this initial conditioning phase, the dogs were placed in a shuttle box—a chamber with two rectangular compartments separated by a low barrier. The floor on one side was electrified, but the dogs could easily escape to the non-electrified side by jumping over the barrier.

Interestingly, the dogs that had been subjected to inescapable shocks in the harnesses didn't try to escape when placed in the shuttle box. They passively accepted the shocks, even though escape was relatively simple. This behavior starkly contrasted with a control group of dogs that had not experienced inescapable shocks. These dogs quickly learned to jump the barrier and avoid the shocks. Seligman and Maier's findings were groundbreaking because they demonstrated that the dogs had learned to feel helpless.

The researchers theorized that having experienced a situation where their actions had no effect on the outcome, the dogs had learned a general rule that they had no control over environmental events. This concept of learned helplessness was later used to explain why people stay stuck in unresolved trauma. These individuals feel a pervasive sense of powerlessness and resignation, affecting their mental health and behavior in various contexts.[6]

When I read about this experiment for the first time, tears streamed down my face. As uncomfortable as this study was to read, it explained a lot and gave me compassion toward myself and others in similar situations. I realized I hadn't left my own situation because trauma had affected my ability to see clearly. Learned helplessness conditions you to believe you are powerless to change your situation, despite having the ability to do so.

> Learned helplessness conditions you to believe you are powerless to change your situation, despite having the ability to do so.

The repeated exposure to uncontrollable and painful experiences teaches you to accept your fate passively, only deepening the trauma. This learned helplessness can keep you, as it did me, trapped in a traumatic situation for years, unable to see a way out or take action, even when it might be possible.

As an entrepreneur and business leader, you're accustomed to navigating challenges and steering your path with confidence.

But when you are in the midst of trauma, or it goes unresolved, it seeps into the very fabric of your being, making you feel like control is slipping through your fingers.

Let's dive deeper into a few more reasons why this happens.

1. **Trauma Alters Brain Function:** When trauma remains unprocessed, it fundamentally changes how your brain functions. (Remember how I explained my brain scan looked notably different with the center area lit up.) This again is when the amygdala, the part of your brain that processes fear and emotional responses, becomes hyperactive. This heightened state of alertness can leave you feeling on edge, as though danger lurks around every corner.

   On the other hand, the prefrontal cortex, responsible for rational thought and decision-making, can become underactive. This imbalance makes it difficult to manage emotions, leading to a constant sense of being overwhelmed and out of control.

2. **The Chronic Stress Response:** Living with unresolved trauma often means living in a state of chronic stress. Your body's natural response to stress—the fight, flight, or freeze reaction—is meant to be temporary. However, trauma can keep this response activated.

   This ongoing hypervigilance drains your energy and mental resources, making it challenging to feel calm and grounded. Instead of being in control, you might feel like you're perpetually reacting to crises, real or perceived.

3. **Emotional Dysregulation:** One of the hallmarks of unresolved trauma is emotional dysregulation. You might experience intense mood swings, irritability, or

emotional outbursts. These emotional highs and lows can make it difficult to maintain your composure in stressful situations, further undermining your sense of control. It's as if your emotions have a mind of their own, steering you away from the calm, collected demeanor you strive to project.

Understanding why unresolved trauma makes you feel like you have no control is the first step toward reclaiming your power.

You Have a Choice

In my bedroom that day, feeling trapped and at a complete loss, I prayed a prayer of desperation, "God, how can I keep doing this? How can I be both Mom and Dad to my kids, lead my company, and keep it all together? Please help me.

In that moment, I remembered that I wasn't alone. Despite these horrible circumstances, God was there with me all along and would be there to give me the strength I needed.

I realized I had a choice to make. I could let the situation completely derail me or choose a different perspective. So, even though I had been knocked down, I could get back up, put one foot in front of the other, and keep going. I relate to the quote by Martin Luther King Junior, "If you can't fly, run. If you can't run, walk. If you can't walk, crawl. But keep moving."

Move I did, and my mantra became "for my girls." I even changed my computer password to this, so I would type it in as a reminder to myself every day. I made the decision to be optimistic and grateful for my family and friends who supported me, a successful business that sustained and challenged me, and my beautiful children who needed me.

Despite what I had been through, I made the decision to take back my life. It's the first step to the healing process, and you can do it too. Recognizing the pattern of learned helplessness along with the other effects of trauma is enlightening and crucial. It allows you to reclaim your power and make proactive changes, ensuring that past traumas do not define your future decisions and successes.

We have explored in Part One the rampant problem of unresolved trauma in today's world, especially in the life of a business leader, and why it's so crucial for us to acknowledge, address, and understand the problem.

My hope is that you have gained awareness of how trauma has impacted your own life and leadership as well as given you the immense desire and belief that you *can* take back control and reclaim your power.

Now as we go on to the next section, Part Two will provide proven success strategies to confront and ultimately heal your past trauma. You will also learn how to build resilience and improve your health for the rest of your life.

Are you ready to begin your healing journey and unlock a healthier, happier you? Let's dig in.

Chapter Reflection—The Five-Minute Empowerment Visualization

1. **Find a Quiet Space.** Begin by finding a quiet place where you won't be interrupted. This could be an office, a quiet corner, or even a park.

2. **Breathe Deeply.** Sit comfortably and close your eyes. Take three deep breaths, inhaling through your nose and exhaling through your mouth. Let go of any tension in your body.

3. **Visualize a Past Success.** Think of a time when you felt truly empowered and successful. It could be a business achievement, a personal victory, or even a simple moment when you felt truly alive and vibrant.

4. **Feel the Emotion.** Dive deep into that memory. What were you wearing? Who was there? What were the sounds around you? Most importantly, how did you feel? Try to recreate that emotion, letting it flood your body.

5. **Positive Affirmation.** While immersed in that emotion, repeat a positive affirmation to yourself three times. It could be something like, "I am capable of great things," or "I hold the power to shape my destiny."

6. **Ground Yourself.** Slowly bring yourself back to the present moment. Feel your feet on the ground and your hands on your lap and take another three deep breaths.

7. **Commit to Action.** Open your eyes and quickly jot down one action you'll take today to channel that feeling of empowerment and success. It could be tackling a task you've been putting off, making a necessary phone call, or setting a new challenging goal.

Integrating this visualization exercise into your daily routine, especially during moments of self-doubt or challenge, can serve as a potent reminder of your capabilities and potential. Remember, empowerment is as much about mindset as it is about action.

PART TWO
The Practical Application

Chapter 6

Put Your Past in the Past

Instead of letting your past define you, you have the power to reshape your story, emerging from the experience stronger, wiser, and more resilient.

If you grew up in the church as I did, there's a story in the Bible you may have heard many times—the story of Jericho and its mighty walls. It's a story of faith, perseverance, and ultimately, of victory. But one day, as I was sitting in church, this familiar story took on a whole new meaning for me. It was as if I was hearing it for the very first time.

The Israelites, under the leadership of Joshua, were on the brink of entering the Promised Land. But there was one major obstacle standing in their way: the fortified city of Jericho. The city was surrounded by massive walls, seemingly impenetrable—a symbol of the obstacles and barriers that may stand in your way.

God gave Joshua a command that might have seemed strange. He didn't instruct the Israelites to storm the city with brute force or to craft an elaborate plan of attack. Instead, he told them to march around the city once a day for six days, and on the seventh day, to march around it seven times. After the final lap, they were to blow their trumpets and shout with all their might.

It might have seemed foolish, even impossible, but the Israelites obeyed. And on that seventh day, after their final march, the walls of Jericho came tumbling down. The city was theirs. The walls that had stood for so long, representing everything that was keeping them from their destiny, were reduced to rubble in an instant.

As I sat there, listening to this story, something clicked. The walls of Jericho didn't just come down—they stayed down. The Israelites weren't worried about the walls coming back up again. The victory was complete. God had done it. The battle was over.

This is how you can look at the traumatic events in your life. Like those walls of Jericho, your traumas can feel like insurmountable barriers, keeping you from moving forward. But when you truly decide to let go and trust in the healing process, those walls can come crashing down. And just like the Israelites, you need to understand that once those walls are down, they are down for good.

> The traumatic event is over. It no longer has the power to hold you back—unless you allow it to.

It was on this day that the ideas for this book began to form. I thought of how I had allowed the past to continue to invade my life, without even fully realizing just how much. It was my decision, and my choice, to truly put the past behind me—to call it done, *once and for all.*

As you are here on this journey with me, you may carry the weight of your past traumas, letting them influence your decisions, your relationships, and your vision for the future. But there comes a moment when you have to decide that it's time to stop looking back at the rubble of those walls. It's time to move forward, to step into the new opportunities that await you with confidence and peace.

In the very beginning of the book, we talked about that everything that has happened in your life up to today is part of your story. It is already written. You can't change this part of your story, but you can learn from it and use it to create the next chapter of your life with more intention.

You can *live a better story.* However, in order to do this, you need to first understand the circumstances of your past and how they may be holding you back.

Your Defining Moments

Imagine your life as a timeline, stretching from your earliest memories to the present. To gain deeper insight into how your past has shaped you, I recommend breaking it down decade by decade, reflecting on the defining moments that have influenced who you are today.

In one of my leadership retreats, I guided my entrepreneur group through this exercise, encouraging each person to identify the key events that have left a lasting impact. This process helps illuminate how your experiences, both positive and challenging, have contributed to your growth and can offer clarity as you move forward.

You can do this exercise whatever age you are—twenty, forty, sixty, or eighty. Think about and reflect on the significant events of your life. Many of those will be happy things—your graduation from high school or college, getting your first career job, your wedding day, the birth of a child or a grandchild, or a big win in your business.

But then, inevitably there will be events that are also part of your story that are unhappy. Something happens you didn't expect. Your story takes an unexpected turn—and it completely throws you. Maybe your parents got divorced, you lost someone you love, you found yourself in an unhealthy or abusive relationship, you became estranged from a family member, you lost a job, you fought a serious illness.

The problem with this is—if you have faced something traumatic in your life, it can derail you. All of this can make you want to hunker down, to freeze, to wait.

If you don't deal with it—if you ignore it, if you stuff it down, if you allow it to make you bitter, it can keep you from your best future—the abundant life that God has called you to.

You have learned about one of the most difficult and defining times of my life—one that I have now healed from and put behind me. I made a choice to pick up the pen and write a new chapter.

Now it's your turn. In the second part of this book, I want to help you take a deeper look at the significant challenges of your past in order to confront and ultimately heal your past trauma. You will also learn life-transforming habits to build resilience and improve your health for the rest of your life.

So let me repeat the question I asked you in the beginning: *Is it possible that you are missing out on your best life because of the pain of your past?*

Your past can get in the way of your best future.

But this is not the life you are meant to live. You have an amazing calling for your life. It is time to no longer let past pain or past hurt hold you back from stepping into this abundance.

Looking Back to Move Forward

When you reflect on your life, each season tells the story of who you are. You will find some chapters of your life filled with joy and success, while others may be marked by challenges and pain. But here's the beautiful truth: the pages ahead of you are blank, waiting for you to write the next chapter with intention and purpose.

As you feel the excitement of writing these new chapters, it's essential to first take a moment to look back. Just as you wouldn't drive a car while constantly staring in the rearview mirror, you shouldn't spend all your time focused on the past. However, that brief glance back—like checking the mirror— serves a vital purpose. It allows you to see where you've been, to recognize what you've encountered, and to ensure that you're moving forward with clarity.

To truly put your past in the past, you need to spend time understanding it. This means taking a deliberate and thoughtful look back, acknowledging and addressing the traumas and significant events that have shaped you and doing the necessary work to process those emotions and heal. It's about confronting the difficult memories, understanding their impact, and then integrating those lessons into your life as you move forward.

But remember, the goal isn't to stay stuck in the past. After acknowledging and understanding those past chapters, it's time to shift your focus forward to the blank pages ahead of you.

These are the chapters that are yet to be written—by you. You have the opportunity to decide what comes next, to write a story that reflects the growth, wisdom, and clarity you've gained.

While the past is a chapter in your story, it doesn't have to dictate how the rest of your book will unfold. You hold the pen, and, with it, the power to write a new chapter—one that is rich with intention, purpose, and the promise of what's to come.

Embracing Post-Traumatic Growth—A New Perspective

You are doing the demanding work of addressing your past, and I understand the courage this takes. It's easy to focus on the stress and emotional toll that trauma brings—what is often described and diagnosed, as it was for me, as post-traumatic stress.

But what if I told you that your past experiences, no matter how painful, could be the very catalyst for your greatest growth? This is the concept of post-traumatic growth, and it offers a powerful new perspective on how to transform your past into a source of strength and resilience.

Post-traumatic growth is about finding positive change in the aftermath of trauma. It's the process of turning pain into power, where the very challenges that once threatened to derail you become the foundation for your personal and professional evolution. This isn't about ignoring or minimizing the impact of your trauma. Instead, it's about recognizing that within the struggle lies an opportunity for profound growth and self-discovery.

Rather than being defined by the stress and hardship you've endured, post-traumatic growth allows you to redefine your story, emerging from the experience stronger, wiser, and more resilient. It's about shifting your focus from what's been lost to what's possible.

How Post-Traumatic Growth Can Unfold in Your Life

As you begin to explore the potential for growth following trauma, you may find changes in several key areas of your life:

1. **Increased Personal Strength.** You've been tested in ways that many haven't. Surviving and overcoming your trauma can reveal a strength within you that you never knew existed. This newfound inner strength can give you the confidence to face future challenges, both in your business and personal life, with greater resilience.

2. **Deeper Relationships.** Trauma can change the way you relate to others. You might find that you're more empathetic, more attuned to the struggles of those around you. This can lead to deeper, more meaningful connections with your team, your family, and your peers. It also makes you more willing to seek out support when you need it, knowing that vulnerability is a strength, not a weakness.

3. **New Possibilities and Opportunities.** Trauma has a way of shifting your priorities and opening your eyes to new possibilities. You may find yourself pursuing new directions in your business and exploring interests or opportunities that align more closely with your values and passions. What once seemed like an insurmountable obstacle can become a turning point that leads to new, rewarding paths.

4. **Enhanced Sense of Purpose.** Experiencing trauma often prompts deep reflection on what truly matters. This can lead to a stronger sense of purpose and a clearer vision for your life and business. You might feel a renewed commitment to leading with integrity, giving back to your community, or creating a positive impact in the world through your work.

5. **Greater Appreciation for Life.** When you've been through significant trauma, you understand better than most how fragile life can be. This awareness can foster a deeper appreciation for the present moment, for the small victories, and for the people in your life. It reminds you to savor the journey, not just the destination.

Turning Your Pain into Power

As an entrepreneur or leader, you know that challenges are inevitable. The true measure of your success isn't just in navigating the good times, but in how you rise from the difficult ones. Healing from past trauma begins with accepting your pain as a chapter in your life's story—a part of the beautiful tapestry that makes you who you are. But this chapter is not the end. You have the opportunity to write a new one, on a fresh page, designed the way you want it.

Post-traumatic growth offers the chance to transform the experiences that once threatened to break you into the building blocks of your greatest achievements. Your past doesn't have to define you. Instead, it can refine you, shaping you into a leader who is not only strong but also compassionate, purpose-driven, and resilient. By embracing this growth, you can move beyond the pain of your past and step into a future where your trauma becomes a source of strength, guiding you to lead with greater intention and impact.

Remember the story of Jericho: God's promise to the Israelites wasn't just the fall of a city, but the inheritance of a land flowing with milk and honey. In the same way, overcoming trauma is not the end of your journey—it's the beginning of a new chapter filled with potential, growth, and fulfillment. This new chapter starts with the decision to leave the past behind, to believe that the walls have truly fallen, and to step boldly into the future that awaits you.

As you leave the past behind and step into your best future, remember that the journey forward isn't just about overcoming what's behind you—it's also about confronting the obstacles within you. Even as you move ahead with intention and purpose, there are still hidden barriers that can hold you back: the lies you tell yourself, the doubts that cloud your vision, and the fears that undermine your confidence.

In the next chapter, we'll uncover these internal roadblocks and explore how your mind can sometimes be your own worst enemy. It's time to confront the falsehoods that have taken root in your thoughts and learn how to rewrite the narrative that guides your life. After all, the greatest power you hold is in mastering your mind, recognizing the lies it tells, and replacing them with truth and clarity.

Chapter Reflection—Your Defining Moments

As you close this chapter, take time to reflect on the defining moments of your life. These questions are designed to help you gain deeper insight into how your past has shaped who you are today and to prepare you for the journey of healing and growth that lies ahead.

1. **Identify Key Milestones.** Looking back over your life, what are the significant events—both positive and challenging—that have left a lasting impact on you? List at least three key moments from each decade of your life.

2. **Understand the Impact.** How have these defining moments influenced your beliefs, your actions, and your sense of self? Consider both the positive lessons and the challenges that these experiences have brought into your life.

3. **Recognize Unresolved Pain.** Are there any past events that you find difficult to think about, or that still evoke strong emotions? What feelings do these memories stir in you, and how might they be holding you back from moving forward?

4. **Consider the Next Chapter.** As you prepare to move forward, what would it look like for you to pick up the pen and write a new chapter in your life? What is one specific action you can take this week to begin addressing a past challenge or to start rewriting your story? How can you create space in your life for healing and growth?

Chapter 7

Your Brain is Lying to You

You have a brain that's been conditioned to expect the worst and see danger even in safe situations.

Abbie, a successful CEO I was coaching, had a whirlwind of a day at work and was content to be at home for the evening. With her black lab resting at her feet, she curled up on the couch and turned on one of her favorite Netflix series.

Sometime later, there was a knock on the door. Easily startled, she jumped in surprise. Who could be at the door? She wasn't expecting anyone. Her mind began to race, and her surprise immediately turned into alarm. Abbie thought to herself, "It must be my ex-husband, or he has sent someone to scare me."

By the time Abbie called me, she was having trouble catching her breath. Although the knock at the door had just been a delivery person, she said to me, "My mind is swirling, and I am filled with fear."

She described that she felt through her whole being like something terrible was going to happen at any moment.

That's because trauma plays tricks on the brain.

Unresolved trauma can create a deceptive web of negative thoughts and patterns that often feel like the truth, but they're merely the brain's protective mechanism.

On the phone together, Abbie and I did a calming exercise and talked through the situation. In doing so she realized she was, in fact, perfectly safe. *Her brain was just telling her something vastly different.* You see, a year before she had gotten herself out of a difficult marriage of many years. She said, "I thought I was doing fine, actually feeling really good these days, and like I had finally moved on."

The Impact of Trauma on Your Brain

Trauma significantly impacts the brain, forming negative patterns that can influence your perception of threats in your work and personal life, even when they aren't present. Recent studies have provided compelling insights into how trauma can fundamentally alter the brain's neural networks, significantly impacting perception and emotional responses.

Research conducted by the University of Rochester Medical Center discovered that individuals with trauma have less signaling between critical brain regions like the hippocampus and the salience network.[7]

The hippocampus, which is critical for forming new memories and connecting them to emotions, often shows reduced activity and connectivity in trauma survivors. This disruption makes it difficult for the brain to distinguish between real and perceived threats, leading to a heightened state of alertness and fear even in safe situations.

This is what was happening to Abbie. Remember the pervasive emotions we talked about in Chapter 2? Fear is at the core of a traumatic past.

Another significant study from the National Institute for Physiological Sciences found that trauma changes how the brain forms and keeps fear memories.[8] They looked at a part of the brain called the dorsomedial prefrontal cortex (dmPFC), which helps bring up memories connected to fear. The researchers discovered that trauma creates strong connections in the brain specifically tied to fear. This means that traumatic experiences can build long-lasting fear networks in the brain.

For example, if someone who has been in a car accident hears screeching tires, their brain might instantly trigger a fear response, even if they are safe at home. This happens because the trauma has created a strong link in their brain between the sound of screeching tires and the fear they felt during the accident. As a result, they might feel intense fear or anxiety in situations where there's no real danger, just because their brain has wired itself to react that way.

Understanding these mechanisms is crucial for developing effective treatments to help you heal from trauma and regain control over your life. Along with this, it's important to recognize that today's culture and "always on" business world only exacerbates what has become a habitual pattern for you.

You Have This Constant Tendency

You know, the wonderful thing about God's grace is that he puts us back together again. Sort of like Humpty Dumpty, you know. No matter what you have been through, He can take your broken story and redeem it.

God puts us back together again, life moves forward, but we have this constant tendency—no matter what we have gone through or how much success we have ever had—to buy into a lie.

Even without a traumatic past, it is easy to buy into the lies in today's culture of having to do more and more, and no matter what you accomplish, it isn't enough. You aren't enough.

People today are overwhelmed—either by the circumstances of their lives or the pace in which they are living.

My book *The Success Lie: 5 Simple Truths to Overcome Overwhelm and Achieve Peace of Mind* introduces this problem in the life of the entrepreneur.

One of those lies that we are addressing and taking a deeper dive here is the lie of *I can't overcome my past*. As we discussed in the first few chapters, a large number of us have unresolved pain from our past—and our tendency is to ignore it, stuff it, or pretend it doesn't exist.

But you are ready to address your past, or you wouldn't have picked up this book.

Identify the Lie

The studies we've explored clearly show how trauma can significantly alter the brain's neural networks, creating strong, persistent fear responses that can mislead us into seeing threats where none exist. This hypervigilance, born from past trauma, often spills over into other areas of your life, leading you to buy into various lies and negative storylines you tell yourself.

You see, it is easier to stay in these patterns of suffering and not address what is really going on.

See if any of these story lines sound familiar:

- I am a failure.
- I can't try again.
- I don't think I will ever be happy again.
- I will be hurt again.
- I can't move beyond my past.
- I can't change.
- I am not good enough.
- Everyone has it together but me.

These internal narratives can be incredibly powerful and detrimental. Storylines such as "you are a failure," "you can't try again," or "you can't move beyond your past" are common lies that many of us believe. They stem from a brain that's been conditioned to expect the worst and see danger even in safe situations. These thoughts aren't just random; they're deeply embedded in our psyche due to the traumatic experiences we've endured.

The negative voices in your mind love to remind you of where you are not worthy. I believe the thoughts are often provoked by the greatest Liar, your enemy and mine—you know the one: "He prowls around like a roaring lion, looking for someone to devour."[9]

The Liar takes advantage of your vulnerability, feeding you falsehoods that keep you trapped in a cycle of fear and doubt. Though he may know your weakest spots and biggest hurts and rejoices when you buy into these lies, here is the truth: You do not need to fall victim to circumstances and difficulties that will invariably come your way. Instead, with the right perspective, these times can be teachers and instrumental to your growth.

The Truth: You Have a Choice

The enemy whispers that you are not enough, that you will never succeed, and that your past defines your future. By identifying and challenging these lies, you can begin to break free from their hold and start living a life guided by truth and intention.

In my own story of trauma and abandonment, it became clear that I was looking at a lie straight in the face. The lie that told me:

- That this chapter would define me.
- That everyone would judge me.
- That I would always be alone.
- That my girls couldn't possibly be okay.
- That I couldn't do this.

I made the decision to take back my life. To take back my power. You can do it too.

But it's not easy. It requires first making a choice. You must realize that this particular chapter is just that—a chapter in your story.

Understanding the impact of trauma on your brain helps you see why you might fall into these patterns, but it also empowers you to change. By acknowledging the lies you believe and actively working to replace them with positive, truthful affirmations, you can reclaim your power and move forward with confidence.

Chapter Reflection

Objective: Identify and challenge the negative thought patterns stemming from past trauma.

Set aside five to ten minutes in a quiet space where you won't be disturbed and follow these steps.

Step 1. Reflect on Your Thoughts

Identify Negative Thoughts: Write down one to three negative thoughts you've had recently.

Examples:

- "I am not good enough."
- "I am a failure."
- "I can't move beyond my past."

Step 2. Identify the Source

Consider the Origin: For each negative thought, try to identify its source. Ask yourself:

- When did I first start believing this?
- How does this thought make me feel and act?

Step 3. Challenge the Thoughts

Consider the Evidence: For each negative thought, write one piece of evidence that contradicts it.

Examples:

1. "I am a failure"—List your successes and accomplishments.
2. "I can't move beyond my past"—Reflect on times when you've made progress or overcome obstacles.

This exercise encourages self-awareness and proactive steps towards replacing trauma-informed lies with empowering truths. By consistently practicing these steps, you can shift from a trauma-informed mindset to one of clarity and positive intention.

Chapter 8

Get in Tune with Your Nervous System

Just as a single out-of-tune instrument can disrupt an entire concert, trauma can throw your nervous system out of harmony.

Imagine you are in your office, working through your usual tasks, when suddenly, the fire alarm blares. Within seconds, you smell smoke and see flames flickering down the hallway. Without even thinking about it, your body springs into action. Your heart races, your breathing quickens, and adrenaline floods your system.

Instinctively, you dash toward the nearest exit, your mind sharply focused on escaping the danger. You feel a surge of energy, making you run faster than you ever thought possible. Your body is doing exactly what it's designed to do in times of crisis—mobilizing every resource to ensure your survival.

Once you are safely outside, away from the fire, your body begins to calm down. Your breathing slows, your heart rate decreases, and you start to feel more in control.

Later, as you reflect on the incident, you realize how effortlessly your body responded to the threat. Your autonomic nervous system, operating on instinct, protected you in the moment of danger and helped you regain calm once the threat was gone.

What is the Autonomic Nervous System and Why Does it Matter?

Before I learned about unresolved trauma and its profound effects on my life, I had little understanding of the complex workings of my body. The intricate systems designed to protect me were a mystery.

> Like many, I navigated through life unaware of how deeply trauma could embed itself in my physical and mental being.

Through my own personal revelations and learning experiences, I began to appreciate the remarkable mechanisms within my body, particularly the autonomic nervous system (ANS). At the risk of getting a little technical, I believe it's important to spend time in this chapter providing some detail on how the ANS works. By grasping its role and functions, you'll better appreciate how your body responds to trauma and stress, and how you can leverage this knowledge for healing.

The autonomic nervous system consists of two primary branches: the sympathetic nervous system (SNS) and the parasympathetic nervous system (PNS). These branches work together to help the body manage stress and maintain homeostasis.

The sympathetic nervous system is often referred to as the "fight-or-flight" system—your body's built-in alarm system designed to protect you. When you face a potential danger, the SMS activates, flooding the body with adrenaline and other stress hormones. This process involves several key steps:

1. Stimulus Recognition

The process begins with stimulus recognition. The brain detects a threat through sensory input, such as sight, sound, or smell. This information is processed in the amygdala, a small, almond-shaped structure located deep within the temporal lobes.

The amygdala plays a pivotal role in the SNS activation. It is responsible for processing emotions, especially fear, and is crucial for triggering the fight-or-flight response. The amygdala constantly scans the environment for potential threats, and, upon detecting danger, it sends a signal to the hypothalamus to activate the SNS.

For example, going back to the imaginary situation of being in a building when you suddenly hear the fire alarm go off—the sound triggers the amygdala, which quickly evaluates the situation and decides whether it's a threat.

2. Activation of the Hypothalamus

The amygdala's distress signal is sent to the hypothalamus, the brain's command center for stress responses. The hypothalamus acts as a relay station, communicating with the rest of the body to initiate the SNS. It sends signals through the spinal cord to the adrenal glands, located on top of the kidneys.

3. Release of Adrenaline

Upon receiving the signal from the hypothalamus, the adrenal glands release adrenaline (epinephrine) into the bloodstream. Adrenaline is a powerful hormone that prepares the body for immediate action. This release of adrenaline marks the body's transition into a heightened state of alertness and readiness.

4. Physiological Changes

Adrenaline triggers several physiological changes to optimize the body's ability to respond to danger:

- **Increased Heart Rate and Blood Pressure:** The heart pumps faster to circulate blood more efficiently, delivering oxygen and nutrients to muscles and vital organs.
- **Rapid Breathing:** Breathing becomes quicker and more shallow to increase oxygen intake, which is crucial for muscle performance.
- **Redirected Blood Flow:** Blood is redirected from non-essential functions, like digestion, to vital areas, such as muscles and the brain. This ensures that the body is primed for action.
- **Dilated Pupils:** Pupils dilate to improve vision, allowing you to better assess the threat and navigate your surroundings.
- **Glucose Release:** Energy stores release glucose into the bloodstream to provide immediate fuel for the muscles, enhancing physical performance.

Overall, the entire process from threat recognition to full physiological response seems like it would be lengthy; however, it happens in approximately two to three seconds. This rapid reaction is essential for survival, as it prepares your body to respond to danger almost immediately. In the earlier example of the office fire, there was no contemplation needed on your part—*you run!*

The Parasympathetic Nervous System: Rest and Digest

In contrast to the SNS, the parasympathetic nervous system is often described as the "rest and digest" system. It promotes relaxation, recovery, and the conservation of energy. Once the perceived threat has passed, the PNS helps return the body to a state of calm and maintenance. This is what happened in the building fire example once you were outside of the building and in a place of safety.

This system is crucial for recovery and maintaining long-term health.

The activation of the PNS involves several processes:

1. **Signal Initiation**

   After the threat is no longer present, signals are sent from the brain to the vagus nerve, which is the main nerve of the PNS.

2. **Counteracting the SNS**

   The vagus nerve acts to counteract the effects of the SNS. It slows down the heart rate, decreases blood pressure, and reduces breathing rate. Later on in this book, I will address specific ways you can help stimulate this nerve for immediate calming effects.

3. **Promotion of Digestion and Healing**

The PNS stimulates digestive processes, allowing for the breakdown and absorption of nutrients. Blood flow is redirected to the gastrointestinal tract, and the body begins to repair tissues and conserve energy.

4. **Restoration of Homeostasis**
   The PNS restores the body to a balanced state, facilitating the maintenance of regular functions, such as saliva production, lacrimation (tear production), urination, and defecation.

The PNS is crucial for long-term health and well-being. It ensures that after the acute stress response, the body can recover, heal, and replenish its resources.

The Dynamic Balance: Sympathetic and Parasympathetic Interplay

The sympathetic and parasympathetic systems work together to maintain a dynamic balance within the body. This balance is known as homeostasis. The autonomic nervous system (ANS) functions much like a conductor leading an orchestra, ensuring that every part of your body's ensemble plays in harmony. Imagine each organ and system in your body as a different instrument in an orchestra.

When the conductor is skilled and attentive, every instrument plays in synchrony, producing a beautiful, cohesive performance. However, just as a single out-of-tune instrument can disrupt a concert, trauma can throw this delicate system out of sync.

The Amygdala and Chronic Stress

The amygdala's role in chronic stress is significant. When the amygdala is repeatedly activated by ongoing stress or trauma, it becomes more sensitive and reactive. This heightened sensitivity means that even minor stressors can trigger a full-blown fight-or-flight response, keeping the body in a constant state of alert.

Research has shown that the amygdala's activity is heightened in individuals who have experienced trauma. A study by Maren and Holmes (2016) published in *Nature Reviews Neuroscience* highlighted the amygdala's role in the acquisition and expression of conditioned fear.[10] They found that the amygdala interacts with other brain regions, such as the prefrontal cortex and hippocampus, to form and retrieve fear memories.[11]

Further, a 2023 study by Gill et al. demonstrated that patients with PTSD exhibit increased amygdala activity when exposed to trauma-related stimuli. This heightened activity correlates with the severity of PTSD symptoms, suggesting that the amygdala's overactivity plays a significant role in the persistence of trauma-related fear responses.[12]

This research underscores that traumatic memories can form new, persistent fear-memory networks in the brain, keeping the SNS activated and the body in a state of chronic stress. This is what happened to me, and you may be facing something similar.

Remember in Chapter 1, I shared how a routine SPECT scan revealed my amygdala was lit up brightly. At the time, I felt fine, unaware that the fear center of my brain was stuck in the "always on" position. My insightful therapist, Jessica, helped me understand it with a simple analogy: She held up her closed fist. "When you sense danger, your amygdala acts like an alarm, preparing your body to take action," Jessica explained, opening her hand and spreading her fingers wide to illustrate. "Once you're safe the alarm turns off." She demonstrated by closing her fingers back into a fist. "When danger reappears, the alarm turns back on"—she opened her hand and spread her fingers again—"and then calms once more into a closed fist when safety is restored."

The problem arises when a person faces chronic trauma. Just like your hand in a wide-open position with fingers splayed, the amygdala becomes so accustomed to being on alert that it gets stuck in the "always on" position.

Trauma Creates a Dysregulated Nervous System

This "always on" activation of the nervous system creates a state of chronic stress. Over time your body just gets used to being constantly in a state of alarm. This can lead to a dysregulated nervous system, where the body struggles to return to a state of calm and balance.

Research by the Mayo Clinic highlights that prolonged activation of the SNS, due to chronic stress, can result in various health problems such as hypertension, cardiovascular disease, digestive issues, and mental health disorders, like anxiety and depression. When the body is in a constant state of alert, the PNS cannot effectively restore balance, exacerbating these issues.[13]

When trauma occurs, it disrupts the normal functioning of the ANS. The SNS becomes overly active, keeping the body in a constant state of alert and preventing the PNS from restoring balance. This state of dysregulation can lead to various physical and mental health problems.

The concept of a "dysregulated nervous system" is well-documented. For instance, a Mayo Clinic study found that chronic stress and trauma could result in an overactive SNS, leading to conditions like hypertension, heart disease, and mental health disorders.[14]

You Can Learn to Regulate Your System

Fortunately, there are ways to learn how to regulate the ANS and restore balance. Mindfulness practices, such as meditation and deep breathing, can activate the PNS and help calm the body's stress response. According to research by the American Psychological Association, techniques like mindfulness meditation have been shown to reduce the activation of the SNS and promote relaxation.[15]

In the coming chapters, you will learn more about the benefits of mindfulness and meditation and how you can incorporate these practices. Additionally, we will discuss how regular physical activity, adequate sleep, and a healthy diet can support the overall functioning of the ANS and promote a more balanced state.

I hope this chapter has helped you to better understand the workings of the autonomic nervous system and its response to chronic stress and trauma. By recognizing the signs of a dysregulated nervous system and taking steps to restore balance, you can get your body's ensemble back in tune, achieving a greater sense of control and resilience in your life.

Restoring harmony in your nervous system is only part of the journey. The next step involves addressing the mental patterns and beliefs that have been shaped by past trauma. Just as you can recalibrate your body's responses, you can also heal your brain by changing your mindset.

In the following chapter, we will explore the power of mindset and how shifting your mental framework can lead to profound healing and transformation.

Chapter Reflection—Ten-Minute Body Scan

This ten-minute body scan exercise can help you stimulate the vagus nerve, bringing your autonomic nervous system into harmony and promoting a sense of calm and safety. This practice is designed to help you become aware of physical sensations, release tension, and foster relaxation.

Step 1. Find a Comfortable Position

- Sit or lie down in a comfortable position. Make sure you are in a quiet space where you won't be disturbed.
- Close your eyes and take a few breaths, inhaling deeply through your nose and exhaling slowly through your mouth.

Step 2. Focus on Your Breath

- Begin by bringing your attention to your breath. Notice the sensation of the air entering and leaving your body.
- Take a moment to feel the rise and fall of your chest and abdomen with each breath.

Step 3. Scan Your Head and Neck

- Start at the top of your head and slowly move your attention down to your neck.
- Notice any areas of tension or discomfort. Simply observe these sensations without trying to change them.

Step 4. Move to Your Shoulders and Arms

- Direct your focus to your shoulders. Are they tense or relaxed?

- Slowly move your attention down your arms, all the way to your fingertips. Take note of any sensations you feel.

Step 5. Focus on Your Chest and Back

- Bring your awareness to your chest and back. Notice the rise and fall of your chest with each breath.
- Pay attention to any areas of tightness or discomfort in your back. Acknowledge these sensations and let them be.

Step 6. Scan Your Abdomen and Pelvis

- Shift your focus to your abdomen and pelvis. Notice how your abdomen expands and contracts with your breath.
- Observe any sensations in this area, such as tightness or relaxation.

Step 7. Move to Your Legs and Feet

- Finally, bring your attention to your legs, starting at your thighs and moving down to your knees, calves, ankles, and feet.
- Notice any areas of tension or discomfort. Feel the connection of your feet with the ground.

Step 8. Integrate the Experience

- Take a few more deep breaths, bringing your awareness back to your entire body.
- Notice how you feel after completing the body scan. Do you feel more relaxed or aware of your body's sensations?

Step 9. Return to the Present Moment

- Slowly open your eyes and take a moment to reorient yourself to your surroundings.
- Acknowledge the time you took to care for yourself and bring harmony to your nervous system.

This body scan exercise is a simple yet powerful tool to help you connect with your body, release tension, and promote a sense of calm. Practicing this regularly can help you better understand and manage your physical responses to stress and trauma.

Chapter 9

You Can Heal Your Brain by Changing Your Mindset

You may not even realize you have become used to reacting in a certain way with particular emotions—fear, anger, bitterness... You are accustomed to the suffering and it's comfortable. But it doesn't need to be this way.

Mind over Matter. Apparently, I said this to my kids a lot when they were growing up. We were having a conversation the other day where I asked my daughters what words or phrases they remembered hearing over and over. "Mind over matter" was at the top of their list along with a few others. Do your best. You can do it. Be nice.

When they would get in an attitude funk, complain about being picked on at school, something not going right, or feeling unfair, I would say to them, "Mind over matter." Despite their negative feelings, they could choose to have a positive mindset and not let the situation ruin their day or their week.

Here is the definition from Merriam-Webster: *Used to describe a situation in which someone is able to control a problem, physical condition, etc., by using the mind.*[16]

Mind over matter is not easy. In fact, in times of challenge, it can be very difficult to keep a positive mindset. This doesn't mean you shouldn't feel your negative emotions when they arise—they need to be recognized and validated. However, a positive mindset is more important than you may realize to your brain health and overall well-being.

As you learned in the last chapter, trauma creates a dysregulated nervous system with an unhealthy activation of the sympathetic branch. When you go through a traumatic situation such as abuse, divorce, or an illness that becomes a chronic issue, the amygdala—the alarm system in your brain—stays in the "on" position. In other words, your brain becomes wired to constantly be on alert for danger. Remember, your body is designed to protect you.

Over time, your body gets used to being constantly in a state of alarm. I know this is how it was for me in a twenty-year marriage to an addict—I just didn't know it until many years later.

> I learned that the stronger the emotion and the pain, the more your body focuses on it. It becomes you—it wires into your mind and body, and you begin to think this is the way it will always be. It is "your normal."

I learned that the stronger the emotion and the pain, the more your body focuses on it. It becomes you—it wires into your mind and body, and you begin to think this is the way it will always be. It is "your normal."

This situation of chronic stress and anxiety harms your brain. Health studies show that stress can kill brain cells and even reduce the size of the brain.[17]

There is good news. Positive thinking improves your brain function and enhances your well-being.[18] Research has shown that the brain grows new cells every day. The science is called neuroplasticity and means that the brain has the ability to change continuously throughout a person's life.

With a conscious effort to think positively in response to situations, we can reprogram our brains and change our life. Who wouldn't want that?

What is Neuroplasticity and How It Can Help Your Past

If you haven't heard the term neuroplasticity, it's one you definitely want to know. What exactly is it and how can it help you break free from a traumatic past?

Neuroplasticity refers to your brain's incredible ability to reorganize itself by forming new neural connections throughout life. This is particularly significant for individuals who have experienced significant trauma, as it offers a pathway to heal and rewire the brain from negative patterns ingrained by acute or chronic traumatic situations.

This exciting development about the brain's abilities is relatively new. For many years, scientists believed that the human brain was static and unchangeable after a certain point in development. This outdated view held that the brain you had as an adult was the one you would have for the rest of your life. This view was widely accepted until the 1960s and 1970s.

However, newer scientific research has proven this is not the case. The groundbreaking research that challenged and eventually overturned this old belief began in the late twentieth century. One of the pivotal figures in this shift was Dr. Michael Merzenich, often referred to as the "father of neuroplasticity."

In the 1970s and 1980s, Merzenich and his colleagues conducted a series of experiments demonstrating that the brain could reorganize itself in response to injury or experience.[19] Another significant contributor to the field was Dr. Norman Doidge, whose work and publications, such as "The Brain That Changes Itself," brought the concept of neuroplasticity into public awareness. His writings put together numerous case studies and scientific research demonstrating the brain's ability to adapt and rewire itself even in adulthood.[20]

The Good News About Neuroplasticity

For those who have experienced significant trauma, this is incredible news. Because your brain continues to change and adapt throughout your life, you can, in fact, change your brain and turn off the alarm. You can create new habits that stick. By adopting new reactions and patterns, over time you can build a habit and change your mindset.

Through neuroplasticity you can rewire your mind. Even if trauma or negative experiences have created certain neural pathways, these can be altered and improved through various therapeutic and cognitive practices. One of these developed by Dr. Caroline Leaf, a cognitive neuroscientist, showed that over

80 percent of participants experienced a significant reduction in anxiety and depression symptoms.[21]

Here's what neuroplasticity can do for you:

1. **Rewire Negative Patterns.** As we've discussed in previous chapters, trauma can create deep-seated neural pathways associated with stress, fear, and anxiety. Neuroplasticity offers the ability to rewire these pathways, fostering resilience and emotional stability.
2. **Enhance Emotional Regulation.** Entrepreneurs often face high-stress environments. Neuroplasticity enables the brain to improve its emotional regulation capabilities, helping to manage stress and maintain mental clarity.
3. **Improve Cognitive Function.** Trauma can impair cognitive functions, such as memory, focus, and decision-making. Neuroplasticity allows these functions to be restored and even enhanced through targeted cognitive exercises and positive experiences.
4. **Build Resilience.** A resilient mindset is crucial for navigating the challenges of a business leader. By leveraging neuroplasticity, you can develop and strengthen neural pathways that support adaptability and perseverance.
5. **Fostering a Positive Mindset.** Trauma can skew an individual's outlook toward negativity. Neuroplasticity allows for the cultivation of positive neural networks through practices like gratitude journaling and positive affirmations, promoting a more optimistic and proactive mindset.

The Other Side of Neuroplasticity

While the concept of neuroplasticity brings a world of hope and potential for healing, it's crucial to remember that this very malleability can also work against you if you're not vigilant.

For entrepreneurs who have faced trauma, the brain's ability to adapt means that both positive and negative patterns can become deeply entrenched. Just as you can train your brain to manage stress and process trauma more healthily, it can also revert to old, unproductive patterns if left unchecked.

The brain's adaptability means that you must remain the "boss" of your own mind. The hypervigilance developed during traumatic experiences can be "shut off" through intentional practices and therapies. However, this same brain flexibility means that without ongoing effort, it can easily slip back into a state of hypervigilance in response to new stresses or triggers. This reversion can lead to feelings of anxiety, heightened stress responses, and even burnout if not actively managed.

A study published in *Neuroscience & Biobehavioral Reviews* in 2017 emphasized that the same neuroplastic changes that allow for healing can also reinforce negative behaviors if harmful experiences and thoughts are continually reinforced.[22] This means that the brain's capacity for change necessitates continuous effort in maintaining healthy mental habits.

Don't let this other side of neuroplasticity get you down. Just realize that understanding the dual nature underscores the importance of being intentional about your thoughts and mental habits. This brings us to a crucial point: What you think is incredibly powerful and significantly shapes your reality.

Why What You Think Is So Important

When was the last time you thought about how your attitude and mindset have affected your life?

You have learned just how powerful your mind is and that you can win your mind and rewire your brain to be healthy. Did you know we think between sixty thousand to eighty thousand thoughts a day? That's truly incredible. Though you can't change the number of thoughts, you can change what those thoughts are.

This is one of the cognitive practices you can incorporate to heal unresolved trauma and to build resilience for future challenges. It was a game changer for me, and it can be for you too. What we think is critically important because what we think will lead to what we say, to how we act, and ultimately what our results are. Battles are won and lost in our minds.

> What we think is critically important because what we think will lead to what we say, to how we act, and ultimately what our results are. Battles are won and lost in our minds.

This reminds me of one of my favorite Bible verses that says, "*Don't copy the behavior and customs of this world, but let God transform you into a new person by changing the way you think. Then you will learn to know God's will for you, which is good and pleasing and perfect.*" Only then will our minds be clear enough to serve God and truly reach our greatest potential.

You and I both know, in this life it's not "if" we will face challenges, it's "when."

Although you can't control the conditions around you, you can control yourself, your attitude, and your response. You can choose a positive mindset and a perspective that leads you forward in the life of significance you are creating, rather than one that holds you back.

I did not know about the concept of neuroplasticity when I was sharing the importance of shifting the mind with my daughters. I learned from my own experience; when I allowed myself to ruminate over negative situations, it brought me down. These negative thoughts led to negative behavior that spilled over into other areas of my life. Mind over matter—I told myself. I told my girls. By choosing to have an optimistic outlook despite circumstances, I felt better, and my interactions with others were also better.

My friend, refuse to let past circumstances define your life and your mind any longer. Instead:

- Choose your mindset to begin changing your story.
- Choose a mindset of optimism and abundance.
- Choose to walk every day with God's spirit and view of you.

Track Your Mindset and Win Your Mind

When I started tracking my mindset, it changed my perspective. You begin by making an intentional practice of checking in with yourself to think about what you are thinking about.

As I became aware of what was thinking I would ask myself, "Are these positive, happy, affirming thoughts?" Or was I capturing negative thoughts churning in my mind—ones that were critical, judging, or complaining?

I set an intent to renew my mind—to have more noble thoughts than my head could hold! And to capture any negative thoughts or words and transform them.

The practice I created, a Twenty-One Day New You Challenge, is also found in my Twenty-One Day Life Reset Program. Here's how it works:

Every morning, choose how you want to show up for the day—as an optimistic and joyful person. Throughout the day, check in with yourself, watching for what type of thoughts you are having. When you catch your mind overflowing with positivity and gratitude, note it. Similarly, when you catch yourself thinking or speaking negatively—such as complaining or judging, note this as well. When this happens, make a choice to change your mindset. The next morning, give yourself a score of how you did the day before: a one, two, or three.

1—You won the day with an optimistic mindset. When you caught yourself with negative thoughts, you were able to recognize and shift them.

2—Neutral. You are aware of both positive and negative mindsets.

3—Get back to work. You had a hard day with a negative attitude or you don't remember.

The more you do this, the easier it will become. Because of neuroplasticity, this conscious attention to your thoughts will begin to rewire your mind to respond with optimism. You will create a habit, and, over time, it will become automatic.

Initially after creating this new intention for myself to think and speak positively every day, I scored a number of twos and even threes. But that was okay; I was becoming aware of my thoughts—the first step to change. I continued to practice, and an amazing thing happened. A couple of weeks in, without even consciously choosing it, my mind began to correct negative thoughts—all on its own!

It was during the pandemic, which was a time we all needed a mindset shift.... I remember it was at the point where we were "done with it all" or we certainly wanted to be. It was a challenging time to stay positive. A girlfriend and I would talk on the phone from time to time and commiserate with each other about the latest news. We would vent and complain for a while and then go on with our day.

On this day, I received a call from my friend who began voicing her frustration with the latest news. Automatically, instead of becoming frustrated too, I responded with something positive. I didn't commiserate or complain, and I found I didn't want to. Gracefully, I was able to change the subject, and we had a laugh over something with our kids.

Later that day, my husband said something that would usually activate me, and it didn't. I couldn't believe it. It was working! My brain was creating new neural pathways, and I was excited. My thoughts were being exchanged from:

Judgement	⟶	Understanding
Complaining	⟶	Being Grateful
Negativity	⟶	Positivity
Scarcity	⟶	Abundance

How You Can Build a More Consistent Thought Life

When you change your mindset, you change your life. It has been transformational for me and countless others I have worked with. As you begin to track your mindset on a daily basis, here are five steps to follow to help you take charge of your thinking:

1. **Be aware of your thoughts.** If you are not conscious of what you are thinking and how it is unhealthy, you cannot change it. Be okay to simply sit with your thoughts and emotions. Be curious about them. Identify them.

2. **Realize negative thinking does not serve you well.** When you become aware of your thoughts and how you interpret and respond to them, you will be empowered to take control. You can control your emotional state and choose thoughts, reactions, and behaviors that best serve you.

3. **Let the negative thinking go.** When you are aware of your thoughts, you can learn to hold on to the ones you want and dismiss the ones you do not want. This will take some practice, but it becomes easier with time. The key is to not let the negative mindset take root.

4. **Replace the negative thought with a positive one.** Do your best to let go of the negative thoughts. It can be helpful to write down the negative thought and write down a positive, affirming thought to replace it.

5. **Feed your mind with positivity.** Your brain processes everything so be intentional about filling your mind with positive things. Make sure that what you are reading, watching, or scrolling through on the internet is lifting you up. Think of it as brain food.

Positive thinking looks at the bright side of life and focuses on opportunities versus problems. As you practice this new mind shift, you will get faster at getting yourself back in a positive mindset. When you think positively you can overcome more. You can achieve more. Your future will be better than your past.

Integrating neuroplasticity and positive thinking can have profound effects on your brain's healing process. By actively engaging in positive thought patterns, you are essentially rewiring your brain to focus on growth and potential rather than fear and limitation. As we've talked about here, this deliberate focus on positive thoughts helps to create new neural pathways, reinforcing a mindset that is resilient, adaptable, and oriented toward success.

When you combine the principles of neuroplasticity with a mindset rooted in positivity, you open the door to transformative change. This combination not only aids in healing from past trauma but also equips you with the mental tools to handle future challenges with grace and strength. As you cultivate this positive mindset, you'll notice an increase in your overall well-being, productivity, and ability to connect with others on a deeper level.

At the end of this chapter, I have included my Twenty-One Day New You Challenge and encourage you to try it for yourself. To have further support, don't hesitate to reach out to me personally or join my Success Life community. (Go to www. thesuccess.life)

Now let's go on to talk about another practice that not only helps to calm an overactive nervous system, but it also brings your body and mind to a balanced, happy place—meditation.

Chapter Reflection

Twenty-One Day New You Challenge

The purpose of this challenge is to choose how you want to show up every day—as an optimistic and joyful person.

Be present and aware of your thoughts and mood throughout the day. When you catch yourself overflowing with positivity and gratitude, note it. Similarly, when you catch yourself thinking or speaking negatively—such as complaining or judging, note this too. Then make the choice to change your mindset.

The more you do this, the easier it will become. You will create a habit, and it will become automatic.

Every day, track your mindset from day before, giving yourself a one, two, or three.

1. You won the day. You had an optimistic, joyful mindset throughout the day. Moments of a negative mindset were brief, and you turned them quickly.
2. Neutral. You were aware of both negative and positive mindsets.
3. Get back to work. You fought a negative mindset all day.

Chapter 10

Meditation Makes a Difference

Be transformed by the renewing of your mind.

Several years ago, I began my own meditation practice by listening to Andy Puddicombe, a meditation and mindfulness expert and the voice of all things Headspace.

I started with the beginner series and a ten-minute guided meditation. The first few sessions didn't go well as I found it nearly impossible to sit still in silence. After one or two minutes I would open my eyes to check the time—*am I done yet?*

As we discussed in Chapter 4, a driven personality will often attempt to *achieve* being present, which simply doesn't work. You will find your tenacity and ability to "push through" when things get tough is a strength than can also be a weakness. In my case, the harder I tried to "accomplish the goal" of meditating the worse I did.

Not one to give up easily, I kept going. In time, the minutes went faster, and I was able to keep with the routine until the helpful voice of Andy Puddicombe would let me know the session was complete.

Andy would say, "How are you feeling right now?" There were times where I didn't feel any different.

However, as I continued the new habit, with a bit of wonder, I began to find that more times than not, I felt better, calmer, and clearer-minded.

I didn't know then I was starting a habit that would become as automatic as brushing my teeth in the morning, and one that would make a profound difference in my life.

Healing Unresolved Trauma Through Meditation

When you're an entrepreneur or business leader, especially one who's faced trauma, the relentless pace of life can often seem like it's working against you. You're constantly pushing forward, always striving, and frequently too focused on the next goal to ever truly sit with yourself.

> But here's a reminder again of the truth that often gets overlooked: true healing from trauma, especially unresolved trauma, doesn't come through pushing harder; it comes through finding peace within yourself.

One of the most effective tools for this is meditation.

Meditation is not just a trendy practice; it's a deeply transformative process that can help you regain control over your life. It allows you to sit with yourself, to explore your inner world in a way that promotes healing and resilience. When you meditate, you're creating a sacred space where your mind can finally rest from the chaos of life. You're allowing your body to engage in its natural healing processes.

The Science Behind Meditation and Trauma

One of the key aspects of trauma is how it impacts the brain. As we've discussed, trauma can cause the brain's alarm system—primarily the amygdala—to stay on high alert, leaving you in a state of chronic stress and hypervigilance. This "always on" state is exhausting and leaves little room for healing. Meditation offers a way to quiet this alarm system.

A study published in *NeuroReport* by Harvard neuroscientist Sara Lazar and her team found that regular meditation can actually shrink the amygdala. The study showed that after an eight-week mindfulness meditation program, participants experienced a reduction in the size of their amygdala, which is responsible for triggering the body's stress response. This change correlated with a reduction in stress levels, suggesting that meditation helps rewire the brain for greater calm and resilience.[23]

This is particularly significant for those of us who are entrepreneurs and high achievers. The ability to down-regulate our stress response isn't just a nice-to-have; it's essential. By regularly engaging in meditation, you're not only reducing the size of the amygdala but also strengthening the prefrontal cortex, the part of your brain responsible for executive function and decision-making. This means that meditation doesn't just help you heal from past trauma; it makes you a more effective leader in the present.

The Many Benefits of Meditation

When you practice meditation, it benefits both your body and mind. Meditation is often thought of as a way to reduce stress and improve well-being, but there are several other health benefits that come with getting into the habit.

In addition to healing the brain exposed to trauma, studies have shown meditation can improve immune function and even slow disease progression. A study by the American Heart Association found that people who meditated had better heart health than those who didn't meditate. It supports your heart by changing how you manage stress to lower high blood pressure.[24]

Meditators also had reduced levels of cortisol, the stress hormone, and an increase in telomerase, an enzyme that helps protect your chromosomes.

Here are some specific benefits regular meditation provides:

1. **Regulation of Stress Hormones.** Mindfulness and meditation help regulate the production of stress hormones like cortisol. Elevated levels of cortisol are associated with various negative health effects, which can be exacerbated by trauma. By meditating, you can lower your cortisol levels, reducing stress and anxiety.

2. **Enhanced Brain Function.** Meditation has been shown to affect the brain's structure, increasing the gray matter in areas associated with self-awareness, compassion, and introspection. This can lead to a more resilient brain, better able to cope with the effects of past trauma. Research suggests that these changes improve emotional regulation, allowing you to respond to stress more effectively.

3. **Increased Mindfulness.** Regular meditation practice helps you learn to stay present in the moment rather than dwelling on traumatic past events or worrying about the future. This can reduce the frequency and intensity of triggers associated with past trauma.

4. **Improved Sleep.** Trauma can significantly disrupt sleep, leading to a host of physical and psychological issues. Meditation improves sleep quality by promoting relaxation and helping to quiet your mind before bedtime. Sleep quality was an area I dramatically improved in my own life by incorporating meditation.

5. **Reduction in Physical Pain.** Trauma can manifest as physical pain in the body as we will talk about in Chapter 12. Mindfulness meditation has been shown to reduce perceptions of pain and can be particularly effective in chronic pain management.

6. **Emotional Release.** Meditation can provide a safe space for you to process and release emotions related to trauma. This emotional processing can decrease the power of traumatic memories and associated feelings.

7. **Neuroplasticity.** Mindfulness and meditation promote neuroplasticity, the brain's ability to reorganize itself by forming new neural connections. This ability is crucial for recovery from trauma as it allows the brain to adapt to new ways of thinking and reacting. In Part Two, there is a chapter dedicated to this topic.

Meditation as a Tool for Reconnecting with Your Body

One of the things trauma does is create a disconnect between the mind and the body.

> You may be so used to pushing through pain, both emotional and physical, that you no longer recognize the signals your body is sending you.

Meditation helps to restore this vital connection.

A study by the American Psychological Association in 2016 found that mindfulness meditation significantly improved participants' awareness of their bodily sensations, a concept known as interoception. This heightened awareness is crucial for trauma survivors, as it helps them tune back into their bodies and recognize when they're under stress. With this awareness comes the ability to respond appropriately, rather than reacting out of a place of fear or pain.[25]

When you meditate, you're training your brain to stay in the present moment. This mindfulness helps you become more attuned to your body's needs and signals. Over time, this practice can lead to a more harmonious relationship with yourself, reducing the symptoms of trauma and creating space for healing.

Trauma can leave you with a heightened sensitivity to stress and an inability to regulate your emotions. This can make everyday challenges feel overwhelming, causing you to react in ways that aren't aligned with your values or long-term goals. Meditation helps you develop a greater capacity to manage your emotions, making it easier to navigate the difficulties of life with a sense of calm and clarity.[26]

For entrepreneurs dealing with unresolved trauma, this is a game-changer. Emotional regulation is key to making sound decisions, building strong relationships, and maintaining your mental health. By incorporating meditation into your daily routine, you're giving yourself the tools to manage stress in a way that supports your long-term success.

Practical Benefits for the Entrepreneur

For those of us in the entrepreneurial world, the benefits of meditation extend beyond just personal well-being. When your mind is clear and your emotions are balanced, you're better equipped to lead your team, make strategic decisions, and navigate the inevitable challenges that come with running a business.

Research has found that regular meditation practice improved participants' resilience, decision-making abilities, and overall mental health. These benefits translated into better business outcomes, as the entrepreneurs were able to approach challenges with a calm, focused mindset.[27]

As an entrepreneur who has faced trauma, you may feel like you're constantly running on empty, just trying to keep up with the demands of your business and your personal life. Meditation offers a way to refill your tank, so to speak. It gives you the mental and emotional resources you need to not just survive but also thrive.

Why Christians Should Meditate

Meditation is often misunderstood, particularly in Christian circles, so I want to address it briefly here. When discussing my book, *The Success Lie*, with a respected publishing agent, the topic of meditation came up. He expressed concern about my open discussion of meditation, especially since I mentioned following a Buddhist monk's teachings. He felt this conflicted with my Christian faith.

While everyone is entitled to their opinion, I respectfully disagree. I firmly believe that Christians can and should meditate. Here's why:

God is sovereign. He is God over all things, including our hearts. Meditation is simply a tool to connect with your inner self and listen to the guidance of the Holy Spirit. It's about doing the inner work necessary to become the person God intended you to be.

Yes, meditation has roots in Eastern religions, and many Buddhists, along with followers of other faiths, practice it. But for those of you who are Christians and may have reservations, let me share what I've learned. Growing up in a conservative household, I was taught that meditation was "new age" and not for Christians. However, when I discovered its benefits for trauma recovery and general well-being, I decided to explore it with an open mind.

The Bible mentions meditation over twenty times, with several occurrences in the Psalms alone. One verse encourages us to meditate on the word of God all day long."[28] So, when you meditate, you can focus on God's word and the fruits of the Spirit—joy, peace, and all the qualities Jesus exemplified during his time on earth.

Some people get hung up on the term "meditation" and find it off-putting. If I say, "I'm going to pray," that's acceptable, but if I say, "I'm going to meditate," it somehow raises concerns. To me, this is just semantics. Both practices involve inner work and self-reflection.

My journey with meditation began as a way to calm my mind—a practice supported by research. Through meditation and breathing exercises, I learned to focus on my breath and let thoughts pass by. This simple practice has grown from a few minutes a day to twenty or thirty minutes, and it has transformed my life.

You can meditate anywhere—in your morning quiet place, between meetings, or after a workout. We discussed the importance of being present in Chapter 4, and meditation is a powerful way to achieve that. If your mind is preoccupied with the day's worries, you miss the beauty of life and the wonders of God's creation surrounding you.

In conclusion, no matter what your faith, meditation is a valuable tool that can help you live the full, abundant life you're called to.

How to Start Your Own Meditation Practice

If you're new to meditation or find it challenging to sit still, start small. Even five minutes a day can make a difference. There are many types of meditation practices, from sitting in the quiet, to listening to music, to using guided meditations where you simply follow along—explore what works best for you.

Consider setting aside a specific time each day for meditation, whether it's first thing in the morning or just before bed. I have found the beginning of the day best for me and have incorporated meditation as part of my morning Success Ritual. You can also incorporate mindfulness practices into your daily routine, such as taking a few deep breaths before a meeting or focusing on your breath while you're stuck in traffic.

There are also several apps available that can guide you through meditation practices, making it easier to get started and stay consistent. Check out the resource section of the book to learn more about these.

How to Meditate with Your Eyes Open

One of the ways to carry your ability to be present throughout the day is to incorporate mindful activities. These are activities where your sole purpose is to be present in whatever it is you are doing—like meditating with your eyes open!

On one of our Success Life retreats, I took a group of entrepreneurs on a meditation walk. On an easy hike in the vibrant hills of Scottsdale, Arizona, it was a wonderful time to be present and experience the moment.

If you would like to try a meditation walk, one helpful method is the five senses approach. Use the five senses of sight, touch, sound, smell, and taste to orient yourself to the present moment and appreciate the world around you at the same time.

1. **What do you see?** Look around as you walk and identify five objects that you see. If you have walked this path a hundred times in the past, try to look for something new you haven't seen before. There's a nest in that bush; that flower is about ready to bloom; a sweet little girl just passed by; the sky is an amazing blue today; that tree must be over one hundred years old.

2. **What do you feel?** As you walk, notice four things that you feel, such as the breeze on your face, the warmth of the sun, the sensation of your clothes on your skin, or your feet hitting the ground with each step.

3. **What do you hear?** You will likely be amazed at the number of sounds there are when you really stop to listen. Identify and focus on one sound at a time until you come up with three.

4. **What do you smell?** Tune out your other senses and isolate the sense of smell. Breathe in through your nose and identify two things.
5. **What do you taste?** Finally, name one thing you can taste—like the mint of the gum you are chewing.

Since our meditation walk, one of my clients said she can better "stay in the moment." She recognized when her mind wandered and thought about something I had said during our walk—"Feel your fingers." It helped her to remember and orient herself to the present.

The more you practice meditation and other techniques to be present in the moment, the easier it becomes. You will become aware more quickly when your mind has drifted and bring yourself back to the moment.

Being mindful in the moment is where you want to be. Be fully present, fully alive, and enjoy the here and the now.

As you navigate your healing journey, it's important to remember to tend to your internal landscape. It may feel impossible at first to release the control and your usual way of pushing through. But it's worth it. Give yourself permission to pause, to be present, to let go.

Meditation in Your Journey to Wholeness

> You have learned the journey of healing from unresolved trauma is not a sprint; it's a marathon. It requires patience, persistence, and the willingness to sit with yourself, even when it feels uncomfortable.

Meditation offers a lifeline in this process. It helps you reconnect with your body, regulate your emotions, and rewire your brain for resilience and calm.

Remember, this may feel counterintuitive at first. You're used to pushing through, to tackling problems head-on, but healing requires a different approach. It requires you to slow down, to be present, and to give yourself the space to heal.

As you continue on your journey of healing, I encourage you to make meditation a regular part of your routine. It's one of the most powerful tools you have to take back control of your life, to move from a place of surviving to thriving, and to create a future that is not defined by your past but by your strength, resilience, and determination.

Chapter Reflection—A Simple Christian Meditation Practice

As we've explored in this chapter, meditation can be a transformative practice, helping you renew your mind and align your thoughts with God's purpose for you. To help you get started, I've put together a simple meditation exercise that you can integrate into your daily routine. This practice will guide you in focusing on the presence of God and inviting positive thoughts and feelings, such as joy, peace, and gratitude, into your heart.

Step 1. Find a Quiet Space

Begin by finding a quiet space where you won't be disturbed. It might be a peaceful corner of your home, a serene spot in nature, or any place where you feel comfortable and relaxed.

The key is to choose a location where you can focus without distraction.

Step 2. Set Your Intention

Before starting, take a moment to set your intention for this meditation. You might say a simple prayer, asking God to renew your mind and fill you with His presence. You could pray, "Lord, I come to You with an open heart. Help me to be transformed by the renewing of my mind as I meditate on Your word and embrace Your peace."

Step 3. Focus on Your Breath

Sit comfortably with your back straight, hands resting gently in your lap, and close your eyes. Take a few deep breaths, inhaling slowly through your nose and exhaling gently through your mouth. As you breathe, focus on the sensation of the air entering and leaving your body. Allow each breath to bring you into a state of calm and stillness, preparing your heart for meditation.

Step 4. Meditate on a Favorite Verse

As I mentioned earlier in the book, one of my favorite verses is Romans 12:2 *"Don't copy the behavior and customs of this world, but let God transform you into a new person by changing the way you think. Then you will learn to know God's will for you, which is good and pleasing and perfect."*[29] Repeat this verse or a favorite of yours silently to yourself, letting the words sink deeply into your heart. Reflect on what it means to be transformed by the renewing of your mind and how God's will can bring joy, peace, and purpose into your life.

Step 5. Focus on a Positive Thought or Feeling

After meditating on the verse, choose a positive thought or feeling you want to cultivate, such as joy, peace, or gratitude. For example, if you choose peace, imagine that God's peace is filling every part of your being, washing away any stress or anxiety. If you choose joy, picture yourself embracing a deep sense of joy that comes from knowing you are loved by God. Hold this thought or feeling in your mind and let it grow stronger with each breath.

Step 6. Be Still and Listen

Allow yourself to sit in stillness for a few moments. Let go of any need to control your thoughts and simply be present with God. Listen for His voice, His guidance, and His reassurance. If your mind starts to wander, gently bring your focus back to your breath or the positive feeling you've chosen to cultivate.

Step 7. Close with Gratitude

As you prepare to end your meditation, take a few deep breaths. Offer a prayer of gratitude for this time of renewal and connection with God. Thank Him for the transformation that is taking place in your mind and heart. You might say, "Thank You, Lord, for renewing my mind and filling me with Your peace, joy, and love. Help me carry these feelings with me throughout my day."

Step 8. Carry the Positivity with You

As you move through your day, remember the positive thought or feeling you focused on during your meditation. Let it guide your actions, your interactions, and your responses to challenges. You can return to this practice whenever you need to reconnect with God's truth and renew your mind.

Chapter 11

Just Breathe

*In the simple act of breathing, you unlock
the power to heal, transform, and reclaim
control over your mind and body.*

Imagine a busy workday morning. You wake up, groggy from a restless night of tossing and turning. While getting ready, you think about the day ahead and your long to-do list, the deadlines, and the meetings. By the time you've rushed out the door, coffee in hand, your mind is already buzzing with the stress of the day. You're moving so fast; you barely notice your breath.

On your way to your first meeting, you find yourself stuck in traffic, frustrated by the blare of honking horns. Your jaw clenches, shoulders tighten, and without even realizing it, you hold your breath. It's subtle, barely noticeable, but it's there—your breath caught in your chest, a small sign of your body's response to stress. You don't give it much thought; in fact, you might not even realize it. But over time, this shallow, restricted breathing becomes a habit, a silent response to the chaos and pressure that surrounds you.

Days turn into weeks and weeks into months, as this pattern continues. You get used to it, thinking it's normal—after all, everyone deals with stress, right? Maybe it started with the constant pressure of running a business or a traumatic event left you feeling vulnerable and out of control. Whatever the cause, your body has adapted, staying in a state of low-grade alert, ready for the next challenge.

As a driven leader, you've learned to push through, to power on regardless of the stress signals your body sends. We talked about this tendency in an earlier chapter.

But this pattern of shallow breathing is taking its toll. We've discussed how trauma can keep your body in a perpetual state of fight or flight, draining your energy, increasing anxiety, and compromising your immune system. You might notice you're feeling more irritable and less focused, catching colds easily, or fighting exhaustion despite getting a full night's sleep.

Here's the secret weapon you didn't know you had—the power of your breath.

When you learn to breathe deeply and intentionally, you tap into a profound source of healing and resilience. It's as if you're flipping a switch, turning off the stress response, and allowing your body to relax and recover. The very breath God gave you—the breath that brought you life—holds the key to restoring balance, health, and strength.

> The very breath God gave you—the breath that brought you life—holds the key to restoring balance, health, and strength.

Breathwork as a Path to Healing

Breathwork is a powerful, transformative practice that taps into the body's innate ability to heal and rejuvenate itself. At its core, breathwork involves consciously controlling the way you breathe, using specific techniques to influence your mental, emotional, and physical states. The simple act of breathing, something you do thousands of times a day without thought, can be harnessed to bring about profound healing, particularly when it comes to stress, anxiety, and trauma.

But while breathwork can be incredibly healing, many of us fall into poor breathing habits without even realizing it. These habits—like shallow breathing, breath-holding, or mouth breathing—are often a direct result of stress, trauma, or even modern lifestyle factors like poor posture. And unfortunately, these inefficient breathing patterns can have a serious impact on your health.

The Impact of Poor Breathing on Health

Poor breathing habits, such as breath-holding or shallow breathing, are common responses to stress and anxiety. Research, including a 2023 study published in *Cell Reports Medicine*, highlights how breath-holding significantly increases stress levels, while controlled breathing can reduce physiological arousal and improve mood.[30]

James Nestor, author of *Breath: The New Science of a Lost Art*, studied the widespread issue of poor breathing and discovered how modern lifestyles often lead to inefficient breathing patterns. Stress, sedentary living, and lack of awareness about proper breathing techniques contribute to these chronic habits, which can negatively affect your health in various ways, from increased anxiety to weakened immunity.

Chronic shallow breathing, which often results from these stress responses, has several negative effects on health:

1. Reduced Oxygen Intake: Shallow breathing limits oxygen, leading to decreased oxygen levels in the blood. This affects brain function and energy, making concentration difficult and causing fatigue.

2. Oxygen and Carbon Dioxide Balance: Shallow breathing leads to a disrupted balance between oxygen and carbon dioxide in the body. While oxygen is vital for cellular function, carbon dioxide also plays a crucial role in regulating blood pH and enabling oxygen release from hemoglobin to the tissues.[31]

3. Increased Stress and Anxiety: Shallow breathing keeps the body in a constant state of alertness, continuously activating the sympathetic nervous system, which can lead to a cycle of stress and anxiety.

4. Weakened Immune System: Chronic stress and shallow breathing suppress the immune system, increasing inflammation and making the body more susceptible to infections and diseases.[32]

How Breathwork Balances Your Body

The negative impact of poor breathing habits, particularly the constant activation of the sympathetic nervous system, highlights the importance of restoring balance to the body. This is where breathwork becomes a critical tool for healing.

One of the most profound effects of breathwork is its ability to activate the parasympathetic nervous system, often referred to as the body's "rest and digest" mode. Remember we talked about the importance of the nervous system, and the parasympathetic branch is the counterpart to the sympathetic nervous system, which governs the body's "fight-or-flight" response.

When you are under stress, the sympathetic nervous system dominates, increasing your heart rate, tensing your muscles, and elevating your stress hormones. This response is helpful in short bursts when you need to respond to immediate danger, but chronic activation can lead to numerous health issues.

Breathwork helps to shift the balance back to the parasympathetic nervous system. Techniques like diaphragmatic breathing (also known as belly breathing), box breathing, and alternate nostril breathing slow the heart rate, lower blood pressure, and induce a state of calm. I will tell you more about these later in this chapter.

By consciously controlling your breath, you signal to your body that it is safe, allowing it to relax and heal. This can be particularly powerful for when you have experienced trauma, as your body remains in a state of heightened alert long after the traumatic event has passed.

How Breathwork Raises HRV

When I began my own trauma healing journey, one of the key health markers I started tracking was heart rate variability (HRV). As I dove into the science behind stress and recovery, I discovered that HRV offers incredible insight into how well your body is managing stress and trauma. Curious about my own health, I decided to monitor my HRV to see what it might reveal about my nervous system.

What I found was that my HRV was on the low side—a clear sign that my body had been dealing with prolonged stress. Initially, I didn't fully understand the significance of this, but after further research, I learned that a low HRV is quite common for those who have experienced ongoing stress or trauma.

As you've learned, trauma, whether emotional or physical, keeps the body in a heightened state of alertness, where the sympathetic nervous system dominates—this results in reduced variability between heartbeats. This essentially means the body struggles to fully relax or recover from stress.

I realized that improving HRV could be a critical marker of recovery, indicating that my body was beginning to heal. If you like to track your health progress like I do, especially in the context of trauma healing, monitoring HRV can be incredibly insightful. It not only shows how your body is managing stress in real time, but it also gives you a measurable way to see progress as you incorporate healing practices, such as breathwork, into your routine.

There are a variety of HRV trackers on the market, and I liked the Lief best. As my breathwork practice deepened, I could track the upward trend of my HRV, reflecting my body's growing ability to regulate itself and recover from stress. Admittedly, I drove my husband bonkers with my deep and often loud breathing—but ultimately, he supported me and I even got him to join me in practice.

As time went on, I noticed a significant shift—not only in my energy levels but also in my heart rate variability. This was a game changer for me. As someone who understands the importance of physical, emotional, and mental resilience, seeing my

HRV steadily improve was proof that the breathwork practice was working. But what exactly is HRV, and why does it matter?

Understanding HRV and Why It's Important

Heart rate variability measures the variation in time between each heartbeat. Rather than having a perfectly regular rhythm, a healthy heart should have slight variability between beats. This variability reflects how well your nervous system is functioning—specifically, how well your body can adapt to stress and maintain balance.

A higher HRV indicates your body is more adaptable and resilient to stress, meaning you're better able to recover from both physical and emotional challenges. On the other hand, a lower or flatlined HRV can be a sign that your body is struggling to adapt and remains in a constant state of stress, which can affect everything from your immune system to your mood and energy levels.

When you have experienced trauma, this imbalance is common as I found out. Trauma keeps the body locked in fight-or-flight mode, with the sympathetic nervous system continually activated. Over time, this leads to lower HRV, meaning the body struggles to calm down, rest, or heal. In fact, trauma can "flatten" HRV, indicating that the body is stuck in a stressed state, unable to fully engage its restorative processes.

So how does breathwork fit into this picture?

Breathwork—particularly dynamic practices like diaphragmatic breathing, SOMA breathwork, or Wim Hof breathing—has the incredible ability to raise HRV. Breathwork activates the parasympathetic nervous system, which is responsible for promoting relaxation and recovery. By engaging in conscious, controlled breathing exercises, you train your body to release stress, balance oxygen and carbon dioxide levels, and return to a state of calm.

Why is this so significant? A rising HRV means that your body is healing. It shows that you're gaining resilience, which is crucial in a fast-paced, high-pressure environment. As a leader, I realized that to show up fully for my team, my family, and myself, I needed to be in a state of balance. Improving my HRV through dynamic breathwork gave me the ability to recover faster, focus better, and handle challenges with a sense of calm.

Higher HRV is also linked to a stronger immune system, better emotional regulation, and even improved cardiovascular health. It's one of the most critical indicators of overall well-being, making it a metric worth paying attention to, especially if you're looking to heal from trauma.

Building Resilience, Health, and Well-Being

Beyond its role in healing trauma, breathwork can also be a powerful tool for building resilience and maintaining health. Regular practice of breathwork strengthens the respiratory system, increases lung capacity, and improves oxygen exchange. This not only enhances physical endurance but also boosts cognitive function and emotional stability. Proper breathing ensures that your body and brain receive adequate oxygen, which is essential for energy production, focus, and overall vitality.

> Beyond its role in healing trauma, breathwork can also be a powerful tool for building resilience and maintaining health.

Breathwork is not just about physical health; it is also a powerful tool for emotional well-being. By helping to release stored emotions and calming the mind, breathwork can reduce feelings of anxiety and depression. It fosters a sense of inner peace and connection, which is essential for healing. Breathwork can also enhance self-awareness, helping you to connect more deeply with your thoughts and emotions, and gain insight into your patterns of behavior.

This regular practice of checking in with myself, noticing when stress was building in my body, and using my breath to calm myself down made a profound difference in my life. So much so, that I started to notice when others around me were not breathing properly.

One example was when we were out with family on our boat in the San Juan Islands when the wind picked up quite suddenly. The boat lurched and tipped abruptly to the side and a couple of items, not secured well, tumbled to the floor with a loud crash.

My grandson, seven years old at the time, was terrified and started to panic. I could tell he was not breathing properly and he was working himself into a panic attack. Instinctively I sat by him and said, "Just breathe sweetheart." He looked at me with wide eyes, not understanding.

I held his hand, put it to his chest and said, "Look at me honey. I want you to breathe in through your nose and feel your chest expand under your hand. Feel that?" He nodded, still shaky and crying. "Now, let that breath go out through your mouth like this."

I demonstrated with a loud ahhh.... Then we began to count together, breathing in through the nose—one, two, three, four—and out through the mouth—one, two, three, four.

To his amazement, in less than a minute, he calmed down, and his breathing returned to normal.

Practical Breathwork Techniques

To start incorporating breathwork into your daily routine, consider these simple techniques:

- **Diaphragmatic Breathing (Belly Breathing):** Sit or lie down in a comfortable position. Place one hand on your chest and the other on your belly. Inhale deeply through your nose, allowing your belly to rise, then exhale slowly through your mouth. Focus on making your exhalation longer than your inhalation. Repeat for several minutes.
- **Box Breathing:** Inhale through your nose for a count of four, hold your breath for a count of four, exhale through your mouth for a count of four, and hold your breath again for a count of four. Repeat this cycle for a few minutes. Box breathing helps to calm the mind and bring a sense of balance.
- **Alternate Nostril Breathing:** Sit comfortably and close your right nostril with your right thumb. Inhale deeply through your left nostril, then close the left nostril with your right ring finger. Open the right nostril and exhale through it. Inhale through the right nostril, close it, and exhale through the left. Continue alternating for several minutes.
- **Wim Hof Breathing:** Sit or lie down in a relaxed position. Inhale deeply through your nose or mouth, filling your lungs completely, and then exhale without force.

Repeat this for thirty to forty cycles, focusing on deep, full inhales and natural, passive exhales. After the last exhale, hold your breath for as long as it is comfortable. When the urge to breathe returns, inhale deeply and hold for ten to fifteen seconds before releasing. Repeat for three or four rounds. This method helps increase oxygen levels and build resilience to physical and mental stress.

- **SOMA Breathwork:** Inhale deeply through your nose for a count of two, then exhale through your mouth for a count of four, keeping the rhythm steady. Continue this pattern for three to four minutes. After several cycles, exhale fully and hold your breath on the exhale for as long as possible. Once ready, inhale deeply, hold for a few seconds, and begin the cycle again. SOMA breathwork helps boost energy and release emotional blockages, encouraging deep relaxation and emotional clarity.

You can learn how to do these breathing practices and more in guided sessions with me on my YouTube channel @ janelle.bruland.

Enhancing Meditation Practice

While breathwork and meditation are closely related, they serve different purposes. Meditation helps quiet the mind and observe thoughts without judgment. Breathwork is more active, using specific techniques to influence your physical and emotional state. By consciously changing the rhythm and depth of your breath, you tap into your body's natural ability to heal and regulate itself.

Incorporating breathwork into your meditation practice can greatly enhance its effectiveness. While meditation helps to quiet the mind and foster a state of mindfulness, breathwork actively engages the body, making it easier to enter a relaxed state. Starting with a few minutes of conscious breathing before meditation can help you center yourself and prepare your mind and body for a deeper meditative experience. I have found this to be extremely helpful in my own practice.

As you become more familiar with breathwork, you may find that different techniques resonate with you at different times. Some days you may need the calming influence of diaphragmatic breathing, while other times you may benefit from the energizing effects of a more vigorous breathwork practice. The key is to listen to your body and use breathwork as a tool to support your needs in the moment.

The Path to Wholeness

Breathwork is a journey—a path to reconnect with your body, calm your mind, and heal your spirit. It empowers you to take control of your physical and emotional well-being, offering a way to release the hold that trauma and stress have on your life. By cultivating a regular practice of breathwork, you can begin to heal from the inside out, finding peace, balance, and resilience.

Imagine being able to navigate your day with a sense of calm and clarity, feeling in control even when the pressure mounts. By harnessing the power of your breath, you can transform stress into strength, anxiety into focus, and fatigue into vitality.

It's time to reclaim your breath, to let it do what it was designed to do—nourish, heal, and empower you.

It's the secret weapon that we all have access to, waiting to be unlocked. Just breathe.

Chapter Reflection

Here are some simple reflection questions to pause, reflect, and engage more deeply with the practice of breathwork.

1. **How often do you notice your breath throughout the day?**

    Reflect on times when your breath may have become shallow or restricted. What triggers these changes, and how does it affect your mental and physical state?

2. **When was the last time you intentionally took a deep breath?**

    Think about a recent moment of stress. How did your body respond? What might have changed if you had paused to focus on your breathing?

3. **What does your breath feel like when you are calm and relaxed?**

    Consider the difference in your breathing patterns during moments of peace versus moments of stress. What physical and emotional shifts do you notice?

4. **How does the idea of using your breath as a tool for healing resonate with you?**

    Do you see your breath as a potential resource for healing? How might focusing on your breath help you navigate stress or unresolved trauma in your own life?

5. **What is one breathwork technique you feel drawn to practice?**

Reflect on the various breathwork techniques discussed in the chapter. Which one resonates most with you, and how can you integrate it into your daily routine?

Chapter 12

Get Your Body on Board

*Remember, this isn't about squeezing in fitness
wherever it fits; it's about making a conscious
decision to prioritize your health.*

It happened again. I was out to dinner with friends, and my
stomach cramped up so bad I had to excuse myself and go
out to the car. This had become a familiar drill—digging in my
purse on the way out to grab the pack of Rolaids I always had
on hand. Then, getting to the car and laying the seat back as far
as it could go, I would attempt to massage the pains away.

It took me ten years on prescription acid reflux medicine
without any relief to finally *really listen* to my body—which
obviously wasn't happy. It was a long journey to the answers
that I am sharing here in this book. As we talked about in the
first chapters, when you don't effectively deal with traumatic
situations in your life—if you stuff them, ignore them, or tell

| 135

yourself you are fine—the pain will show up somewhere. For me, it showed up physically in my stomach.

In Dr. Bessel van der Kolk's renown book, *The Body Keeps the Score*, he describes how trauma can manifest physically in the body, causing symptoms like stomach aches, back pain, headaches, and many others.[33] He explains that these physical symptoms are often the body's response to unresolved emotional distress, highlighting the deep connection between the mind and body in processing trauma. This concept underscores the importance of addressing both psychological and physical aspects when healing from trauma.

Trust Yourself Over the Experts

When my stomach issues got to a point where they were interfering with my day-to-day activities, I sought medical help—first my family doctor, then a specialist who happened to be a renowned gastroenterologist in our area. He conducted several tests including a comprehensive study in the hospital where they observed me digesting a meal. The ultrasound revealed that I had an inflamed esophagus and was subsequently diagnosed with severe acid reflux.

The doctor wrote me a prescription for Omeprazole and sent me on my way. He said this would fix the problem; however, I would need to stay on this medication to keep the issues at bay. I never thought to question his prognosis or course of action. After all, *he was the expert*. And it did take care of the problem—for a while. I continued to struggle with stomach issues periodically and experimented with various medications to combat it.

However, I didn't realize until years later that the acid reflux prescription was a band aid versus healing the problem, and it was actually blocking the acid my stomach needed to properly digest food. Frustrated to be on any medication and having the desire to be free of them, I went the non-conventional route to a naturopathic physician. She conducted a food allergy test which showed sensitivity and inflammation in response to a variety of foods. I won't go into all the detail here, but this is the bottom line: I wasn't giving my body the proper nutrition it needed for me to be my best.

In fact, I was giving it a lot of the wrong things every day— such as casein (a protein found in cow's milk), which I am overly sensitive to. My naturopath recommended reducing or going off dairy all together, as that would likely take care of my stomach issues. What happened over the course of the next few months felt like a miracle cure, and, within a year, I was able to get completely off the acid reflux medication. Now, several years later, I've never used it again.

Trauma Plays a Significant Role in Your Health

If you are struggling with health issues as I did, understand that trauma can play a role.

Recent studies emphasize the profound impact of trauma and chronic stress on health. I am sure you have heard that "stress can make you sick."

For instance, a study highlighted by the American Psychological Association in 2023 revealed that long-term stress can precipitate a wide array of health issues, including hypertension, heart disease, and mental health conditions like anxiety and depression. This research underscores the importance of addressing trauma not just for mental well-being but also to prevent a myriad of physical health problems.[34]

It's also important to note that you might experience physical symptoms in direct response to your emotional state. I was fascinated to learn about the work of Franz Alexander, a pioneering figure in psychosomatic medicine. His research published in 1950 suggests that unresolved emotional conflicts can manifest as physical symptoms, a theory that resonated with the idea that the mind could create physical conditions based on psychological states.[35] His theories paved the way for recognizing the integral relationship between the mind and body.

These concepts emphasize why it's critical to get your body on board. The holistic approach of your mind and body—both psychological and physical—is a key to your healing and the improvement of your overall health.

Learn What is Right for You and Create a Plan

As medical doctors are trained experts, you expect them to have the answers and trust they will guide you to the best remedy. There are amazing physicians and specialists out there, and I have had some of the most wonderful and compassionate care from traditional medicine experts. I truly believe that good doctors have the best intentions, but at the end of the day, the best expert on your body is you. You are your greatest healer.

I urge you to not take your doctor's recommendation as the final answer. I have seen many friends and clients be told they "needed surgery" only to go to another specialist to be told they didn't. My husband Graham is an example: Having injured his knee playing soccer as a kid, he developed pain in his forties that became unbearable. A specialist told him surgery was his only option to repair his MCL. Not desiring surgery, he sought the opinion of a sports physical therapist and good friend who said, "Give me six weeks with you and you won't need surgery." It wasn't an enjoyable physical therapy experience, but Dr. DeRoche healed my husband—without surgery.

Start Now and Prioritize Your Health

In healing trauma, as well as setting yourself up for your best future, you need to focus on taking better care of your "whole body." But first, we need to get a problem out of the way: the entrepreneurial dilemma.

If you struggle to prioritize your health, know that it's a familiar story for many in the business world. You may find yourself relating to these sentiments:

- My business demands are just too overwhelming right now.
- I'm constantly juggling work and family responsibilities.
- I'm always in survival mode with no time for myself.
- I'm starting to doubt my ability to maintain a healthy lifestyle.
- I keep telling myself I'll focus on fitness when things calm down.

This is the entrepreneurial dilemma: How do you balance the demands of your business with the need for personal well-being?

Before diving into specific strategies, it's vital to recognize the fundamental importance of making your health a priority, particularly for entrepreneurs on a journey to heal from trauma. Maintaining optimal health through balanced nutrition, regular exercise, and quality sleep is crucial not just for physical fitness but also for sustaining the energy necessary to heal your body.

As you've learned, there is a profound connection between your physical state and your mental health; taking care of your body is a pivotal step in both healing from past trauma and safeguarding your future well-being. Prioritizing your health is essential to ensure you remain resilient and capable in all aspects of life and work.

Let's discuss the three foundational pillars of health to get your body on board.

Eat to Promote Healing

Through my own trauma healing journey, I realized how critical it was to keep my body in peak health. Nutrition is an area you and I need to take seriously.

In your busy life, you may sometimes find your health and nutrition on the back burner. You may struggle with eating too much, too little, or not the right foods. If this is you, don't wait to prioritize this important health area.

In her best-selling book, *This is Your Brain on Food*, nutritional psychiatrist Dr. Uma Naidoo stresses that our nutritional health is critical to our overall health and the function of our brain. There is an intricate relationship between our gut and our brain, and the foods that we eat will either help us perform better or, conversely when you eat poorly, it will have a negative impact on your mental health and well-being.[36]

This means that you must prioritize nutrition to sustain high performance and truly give your best to those you love.

Get Your Body Moving

Exercise releases endorphins, which are natural mood lifters. They help improve mental health and well-being and give you the ability to tackle business challenges with a positive mindset.

Here are four practical strategies to help you incorporate consistent fitness into your busy schedule:

1. Intentional Scheduling

For entrepreneurs, every minute counts. Just as you meticulously schedule your business meetings, applying the same level of intentionality to your workout routine is essential. The key lies in finding a slot in your day where exercise can become a non-negotiable activity, just like an important client meeting.

Start by examining your daily routine. Are you an early riser, fueled by the quiet of the morning, or do you find your energy peaks in the afternoon? Some find that starting the day with exercise sets a positive tone, while others prefer unwinding with a workout after a day's work. Experiment with different times to see what naturally fits into your schedule without causing additional stress.

Utilizing digital tools can also play a pivotal role. Calendar apps aren't just for business appointments. Block out time for your workouts and set reminders. Treat these time blocks with the same respect you would a meeting with your most important client.

Remember, this isn't about squeezing in fitness wherever it fits; it's about making a conscious decision to prioritize your health.

Above all, be realistic. If committing to an hour daily feels overwhelming, start with shorter sessions. Consistency is more important than duration. Over time, as exercise becomes a habitual part of your routine, you can gradually increase the duration and intensity.

2. Finding Joy in Exercise

The secret to a sustainable fitness routine is finding joy in the activity. Exercise shouldn't feel like a chore; it should be something you look forward to. This might mean stepping out of your comfort zone and trying activities beyond the traditional gym workout.

Consider what makes you happy. Do you enjoy nature? Try hiking or outdoor cycling. Love music? Dance classes or Zumba might be your calling. If competitive sports excite you, joining a local sports league can be both socially and physically rewarding. The possibilities are endless—from yoga and Pilates for those who prefer a more meditative approach to martial arts for an energizing challenge.

Remember, variety is key. Mixing up your workout routine not only keeps things interesting but also challenges different muscle groups and reduces the risk of injury. This approach keeps your fitness journey fresh.

3. The Role of a Fitness Coach

A fitness coach or personal trainer can be a game-changer, especially for entrepreneurs who are short on time and need efficient, effective workouts.

This approach was incredibly helpful for me when I found myself in an exercise slump. A coach offers more than just exercise routines; they provide motivation, accountability, and expertise tailored to your specific fitness goals and physical needs.

When selecting a coach, it's crucial to find someone who aligns with your objectives. Are you looking to build strength, improve flexibility, or train for a specific event? Different coaches specialize in different areas, so choose one who matches your goals. Additionally, a good coach will consider any pre-existing injuries or health concerns, ensuring your workout plan is safe and suitable.

Having a coach also means having someone to hold you accountable. They can track your progress, adjust your workout plan as needed, and push you to achieve your best. This support can be particularly beneficial on days when motivation is low.

My coach Kylie pushes me outside my comfort zone—she has me doing exercises I definitely wouldn't have done on my own (*frog jumps and farmer's carries!*) and I am seeing positive and faster results.

4. Integrating Movement into Daily Life

Incorporating movement into your day-to-day life is a subtle yet effective way to enhance your fitness. It's about making conscious choices to be more active, even during your busiest days.

Simple changes can make a significant difference. For example, if you spend a lot of time at a desk, consider a standing desk or take short breaks every hour to stretch or walk. Instead of sitting through phone calls, make them walking meetings. Graham and I schedule walking meetings every chance we get. This not only adds steps to your day but also boosts creativity and focus.

Family activities can also be a great way to incorporate movement. Evening walks or weekend bike rides improve physical health and also strengthen family bonds. If you have young children, playing active games with them is both fun and a great workout.

Additionally, think about how you can make everyday tasks more active. Choose stairs over elevators, park further away from store entrances, or do light stretching while watching TV. These small changes accumulate, leading to significant health benefits over time.

Why Getting Good Sleep Matters

Though I struggled with getting good sleep for many years, I must admit I didn't pay much attention to it.

I remember a particular time in my business when I was not getting much sleep, and it was affecting my work. There was a project deadline looming, and I was having trouble getting my head in the game. Despite my efforts I felt foggy and could not stay focused for long; even the easiest tasks of the day seemed challenging.

"Get it together," I coached myself. In only an hour, it would be time to leave to pick up the kids.

The lack of sleep I was getting was taking its toll. I simply could not shut my mind off at night, and it had become an unwanted routine to wake up at 4 a.m.

"Other high performing entrepreneurs seem to function fine with only a few hours of sleep a night," I told myself.

Today's Work Culture Doesn't Promote Sleep

You may, like I did for a long time, not have sleep as a top priority. It seems that today's work culture values and even brags on those who work too much and sleep too little.

Dr. Matthew Walker, a renowned leader in the field of sleep science puts it this way. "We glorify the high-powered executive on email until 1 a.m., and then in the office by 5:45 a.m.; we laud the airport 'warrior' who has traveled through five different time zones on seven flights over the past eight days."[37]

The same argument you may use for not having time to exercise or prepare the right meals for yourself is also used regarding sleep.

You don't have enough time to sleep because you have so much work to do.

Dr. Walker claims it to likely be just the opposite. He suggests the reason executives still have so much to do at the end of the day is precisely *because* they do not get enough nighttime sleep.[38]

Good Sleep Plays a Critical Role

Good sleep plays a critical role in the healing process from trauma for several reasons:

Emotional Regulation. Sleep helps to regulate emotions and mood, which can be particularly volatile after experiencing trauma. Adequate sleep allows the brain to process emotional information and reduce the intensity of emotions, helping individuals cope more effectively with stress and anxiety.

Memory Consolidation. During sleep, the brain processes and consolidates memories, including traumatic ones. This process is crucial for recovery from trauma as it helps to integrate the traumatic experience into one's life narrative in a less distressing way.

Reduced Hyperarousal. Trauma can lead to a state of hyperarousal, where the individual is constantly on alert. Quality sleep helps reduce this arousal level, lowering stress hormones like cortisol and facilitating a calmer state of being.

Physical Restoration. Sleep is a time when the body undergoes repair and rejuvenation. For someone recovering from trauma, physical health is deeply intertwined with mental health. Sleep supports the healing of the nervous system and helps maintain the health of other bodily systems that can be negatively affected by stress and trauma.

Neuroplasticity: We discussed the benefits of neuroplasticity in a previous chapter, and sleep is one of the ways it is used. Sleep enhances the brain's plasticity, its ability to change and adapt in response to experiences, including traumatic ones. This neuroplasticity is vital for recovery from trauma as it allows the brain to adapt and develop new, healthier patterns of thinking and behavior.

Ensuring regular, restorative sleep is a key component of a holistic approach to recovering from trauma, supporting both physical and mental health improvements.

Prioritizing Health as an Entrepreneur

As an entrepreneur, your health is integral to your business's success. Often, entrepreneurs fall into the trap of prioritizing their business over their health, leading to long-term negative consequences. Prioritizing health is not just about healing from trauma and avoiding illness; it's about cultivating a lifestyle that enhances your capacity to lead and innovate.

First, understand that your physical well-being directly impacts your mental and emotional state. Regular exercise and a healthy diet enhance cognitive functions, including memory, attention, and problem-solving skills, which are crucial in the fast-paced entrepreneurial world.

> Prioritizing health is not just about healing from trauma and avoiding illness; it's about cultivating a lifestyle that enhances your capacity to lead and innovate.

Second, prioritize sleep. As we discussed earlier in this chapter, entrepreneurs often sacrifice sleep for work, but this can be counterproductive. Quality sleep is essential for mental clarity, emotional resilience, and overall health. Develop a regular sleep schedule and create a conducive sleep environment.

Finally, lead by example. As the leader, you set the tone for your organization's culture. By prioritizing your health, you inspire your team to do the same, creating a healthier, more productive work environment.

Embracing a holistic approach to healing from trauma and ensuring a healthier, happier life involves getting your entire body on board. This is more than just a health goal—it's a crucial element of your journey as an entrepreneur.

By prioritizing your physical, mental, and emotional health, you're not just investing in your immediate well-being; you're laying the foundation for long-term success and resilience. This comprehensive care for your body supports your capacity to handle business challenges with greater vigor and clarity, ensuring you can perform at your best in all areas of life.

Chapter Reflection

As you plan your business strategies, include a health strategy too. Your body is your most valuable asset, and taking care of it is essential for sustained success. Whether it's scheduling regular workouts, trying new sports, or simply ensuring you have time for physical rejuvenation, these practices will enhance your personal well-being and empower you to thrive both personally and professionally.

Take a moment to reflect on the three foundational pillars of health: Balanced Nutrition, Regular Exercise, and Quality Sleep.

- Which of these pillars comes most naturally to you?
- Which one feels the most challenging, and why?
- What small, actionable step will you take this week to strengthen one of these pillars in your life?

It's time to prioritize your health and take that first step. Remember, progress is built one intentional choice at a time. You've got this!

Chapter 13

Treatment Modalities to Help You Heal

*You cannot push your way to recovery. You
have to heal your way to recovery.*

What an interesting session it was.... Over the past few
months, I'd been working with a couple of different treatments for resolving trauma simultaneously—neurofeedback
and craniosacral therapy—which you will learn more about in
this chapter along with others.

After a number of sessions together, I had developed a deep
trust with my craniosacral therapist Jenna. Then came the session that catapulted my healing. On that day, I shared with
Jenna my exciting progress with neurofeedback and asked for
her help. While my beta levels—brainwave patterns associated
with alertness and a state of alarm—were starting to decrease,
signifying a reduction in my state of alarm, my alpha and delta

waves were going in the opposite direction than expected. Instead of increasing, which would have indicated greater relaxation and healing, they were actually decreasing.

I asked Jenna if she could help coax my alarm system into further calm and help correct this imbalance. As she gently touched my head, trying to soothe my inner alarm, something surprising happened. She described it as, "Your protector emerged, and it was strong and unyielding—blocking my efforts." (The "protector" she was describing refers to an internal part of us that steps in to shield us from perceived harm, often arising from past experiences of pain or trauma.)

Though admittedly, the conversation itself felt very strange, I decided to go with it. I asked her if she would assure this protector saying, "I am safe. Tell her I am safe now. Will you tell her the girls are safe now?"

She repeated these words back to me, and as she did, I felt the beginning of a release. Tears started to stream down my face, but there was no overwhelming sadness accompanying them. Was it my younger self weeping from the immense challenges I had been through, finally ready to let go? Jenna asked me what I was feeling, and I replied, "Nothing, really."

She nodded, but before our session ended, she held my hand, looking at me with compassion. She told me she sensed a deep shift happening within me, that I was close to releasing it all, but as she coaxed my alarm, she sensed pure terror and decided to pause.

Driving home from my session that day, I thought to myself how strange it is to realize that such intense experiences are happening inside me without my conscious awareness. There's a battle waging within my heart, brain, and nervous system—beyond the occasional tightness in my chest; the anxiety; and the vague, jumbled nightmares I wake up from, drenched in a fear I can't fully comprehend.

My body has been my protector for so long, and I am profoundly grateful for how hard it has worked to keep me safe, even when I was unaware of the trauma I carried. For the past thirty years, my body had been in a state of constant alarm, constant protection, never truly settling down.

With continued work and a commitment to my healing journey, something incredible happened—I began to transform. The unresolved trauma that had been locked inside me for so long was finally released. The layers of protection that my body had built over the years began to peel away, revealing a deep sense of peace and freedom I had never known before.

It felt like a heavy weight lifted from my shoulders, allowing me to breathe more easily and live more fully. No longer held captive by my past, I felt a profound sense of relief and a new lightness in my being. The fears that once haunted me were replaced with a calm assurance. I was safe. I was free. This transformation allowed me to connect with my true self, experience deeper joy, and approach life with a renewed sense of purpose and possibility.

Through what you've learned in this book so far, I hope you are seeing that stepping out of trauma's shadow is not just a possibility, but a doorway to a healthier you, where you too can finally release the deep-seated pain that has long kept you in survival mode. The journey may

> Stepping out of trauma's shadow is not just a possibility, but a doorway to a healthier you, where you too can finally release the deep-seated pain that has long kept you in survival mode.

not always be easy, but it is a path toward freedom and healing, one step at a time.

The Path of Trauma Healing

Navigating the world of trauma recovery can be daunting, especially when you're balancing the demands of your work and home life. Thankfully, the last few decades have brought a change in thinking, and the walls of silence and stigma surrounding mental health are gradually crumbling.

There are now more treatment modalities than ever before to combat and heal your trauma. This chapter will provide insights into a variety of helpful methods, many that I—and my clients—have used with success. This list represents just a sample of the trauma therapies available. It is by no means exhaustive but provides a snapshot of diverse approaches you can explore as part of your healing journey.

In the process of healing my own trauma, I found resources extremely vague and limited (other than the highly recommended use of prescription drugs and psychedelics) and felt like I wandered around in the dark to discover what worked that was natural and safe. That's why I gathered this extensive list for you—to give you hope and a place to start. It is a list I wish I had for my own healing.

As you review the following, please note I am providing a deeper dive into the therapies that I have the most personal experience in. But this doesn't necessarily mean these modalities are any better than the others—they were most transformational for me.

Craniosacral Therapy (CST)

Craniosacral therapy (CST) is a gentle, hands-on approach that focuses on enhancing the functioning of the craniosacral system—the membranes and fluid that surround and protect the brain and spinal cord.

I discovered this treatment while visiting a holistic spa on vacation, and it had such a profound impact that I knew I wanted more. After returning home to Washington, I began my search for a trained therapist and found the lovely Jenna Anderson.

CST is particularly effective for trauma as it helps release tensions deep within the body to relieve pain and dysfunction and to improve whole-body health and performance. This therapy is used to relieve pain, stress, and the side effects of various conditions, including trauma. It works by releasing tension in the body's connective tissues, facilitating better overall bodily function and promoting relaxation and healing.[39] Here's how it can be particularly beneficial for healing trauma:

1. **Releasing Tension.** By gently manipulating areas around the head, spine, and pelvis, CST helps to release the deep-seated tensions caused by trauma, which often linger in the body's fascia.

2. **Calming the Nervous System.** The light touch used in CST can help calm the nervous system, which is often in a heightened state of alert following trauma. This calming effect can alleviate symptoms of anxiety and stress, providing a sense of relief.

3. **Enhancing Bodily Connection and Awareness:** CST encourages a heightened state of body awareness, helping you reconnect with your physical self and address

areas of discomfort or imbalance that may be linked to past trauma.

As I mentioned at the beginning of this chapter, my therapist Jenna was immensely helpful to me in addressing the trauma within my body, and I continue to use CST as a maintenance therapy to manage stress.

Eye Movement Desensitization and Reprocessing (EMDR)

Eye movement desensitization and reprocessing (EMDR) is a psychotherapy technique developed by Dr. Francine Shapiro in the late 1980s. I was told it is particularly effective for individuals who have experienced trauma, so it was one of the first and most helpful treatments that I used.

EMDR therapy is based on the premise we discussed earlier in the book—that traumatic experiences can cause disruptions in the normal adaptive processing of memories, leading to frozen or blocked emotional processing.

The core of EMDR therapy involves recalling a traumatic memory while simultaneously undergoing bilateral sensory input, such as side-to-side eye movements or hand tapping. In my experience with an EMDR specialist, we used a tactile stimulator—a small device that you hold in your hands and delivers vibrations that alternate between the left and right hand. This process promotes bilateral stimulation, a key component that helps to facilitate the brain's natural healing abilities, similar to what occurs during REM sleep phases.

EMDR has been found effective for a range of issues stemming from trauma, including PTSD, anxiety, and depression.

This approach allows the brain to process and integrate traumatic memories into the larger psychological framework in a way that reduces their painful intensity.[40]

EMDR therapy was recommended to me because of the PTSD diagnosis resulting from the brain SPECT scan. It's not for everyone as it does involve recalling difficult memories. However, for me, EMDR was *life-changing*. Not only was I able to process and reconceptualize embedded traumatic memories, such as the day I came home to find my first husband gone, but I also was able to change my relationship with other fears, such as flying.

Though I wasn't afraid of being on a plane in my younger years, suddenly in my late thirties, my anxiety mounted whenever I was on a flight. It got to a point where bad turbulence would bring me to tears as I white-knuckled the armrests.

After successfully working through a handful of traumatic memories with my therapist Jessica, I asked her, "Can EMDR work for a fear of flying?"

She told me it could. Here's how the process went:

First, Jessica asked me to recall a memory of a flight that caused particular distress. I picked my airport experience that I shared with you at the beginning of the book. She then asked me, "On a scale of one to ten, ten being the worst, rate the intensity of your feelings or distress about this specific event."

I answered that it felt like an eight. (This rating is known as the Subjective Units of Distress Scale, or SUDS. It helps the therapist gauge the initial level of emotional distress associated with the memory.)

Then she asked me to walk through the event in my mind as if I was watching a movie. With my eyes closed, I sensed every step of the experience as best I could, from walking down the jet bridge, entering the plane, and finding my seat to getting settled and buckling my seatbelt. Jessica guided me to when the plane entered the storm and the associated emotions. Periodically my therapist would ask questions surrounding my fears and beliefs, along with rating my distress level. As in previous EMDR sessions, my body responded positively, and my level of distress went down.

By the end of the session, my intensity score had dropped dramatically to a two, meaning that the memory had become much less emotionally charged. The true test came on my next flight a couple of weeks later. To my delight, EMDR was successful once again and my usual anxiety around flying was gone, and still is today.

Hormone Replacement Therapy

Trauma can disrupt the body's hormonal balance, leading to issues like adrenal fatigue, where the adrenal glands can't produce adequate stress hormones or other endocrine disorders. Though not a direct treatment for unresolved trauma, I believe it is an important adjacent therapy to consider. Hormone therapy was a game changer for me, particularly as I was premenopausal while working on my trauma healing.

Regardless of your age, but especially if you are over the age of forty, I highly recommend getting your hormone levels checked. Hormone therapy can help stabilize these levels, potentially alleviating some of the mood swings, anxiety, and stress responses linked to trauma.

Neurofeedback

My husband Graham heard about neurofeedback before me while working with a fabulous psychologist and specialist in the therapy, Dr. Nathan Brown. He was seeing Dr. Brown for problems he was having with focus—a common issue for individuals with ADHD.

Neurofeedback, an innovative therapy that harnesses the brain's adaptability, is an invaluable tool for improving overall brain performance, including focus; Graham and I were both extremely excited about this feature. It is also an excellent technique for entrepreneurs navigating the aftermath of trauma. Grounded in the science of neuroplasticity, this therapy offers a sophisticated method to train your brain, enhancing its efficiency and stability through real-time feedback on brainwave activity.

Dr. Brown started by providing Graham with a simple brain assessment that showed what areas of the brain were operating at peak performance and what areas were not. Then he recommended an interactive tool called the Muse, which has a phone app where you can do brain training exercises. After a few months of these trainings, Graham's focus scores improved dramatically from being able to hold focus for three seconds in training to thirty seconds! It was incredible and these results inspired me to sign up.

My first brain assessment showed the need for improvement, especially in the prefrontal cortex area. As we discussed, in situations of chronic stress or trauma, the amygdala can become overreactive. This heightened state can lead the amygdala to dominate the brain's response systems, leading to an imbalance where the rational and calming influences of the prefrontal cortex are diminished. In other words, the alarm is always on.

I was excited to get to work. Dr. Brown gave me specific exercises that I performed every day using the Muse device. Feedback, either visual or auditory depending on the exercise, is provided instantly, showing how your brainwaves fluctuate. As you go through the session, your brain's activity is continuously monitored against specific therapeutic goals. Successful alignment with these goals triggers positive reinforcement, guiding your brain toward optimal functioning.

You'll remember I talked a little about my experience with neurofeedback in Chapter 4. The hardest part can be learning to allow your brain to relax and do the work versus forcing it.

It wasn't an overnight change, but my persistence paid off. I simply incorporated the recommended brain exercises into my daily routine. With repeated sessions, your brain progressively learns healthier patterns and how to sustain a healthier regulated neural state.

Over time, I began to feel different, and better; my energy as well as my ability to relax improved, and I was ruminating less and sleeping soundly. Six months later, I took a second assessment and had brought my brain functions back in balance. Dr. Brown told me my brain was functioning at a high level—and gave me the best news: "Janelle, you have turned off the alarm."

Graham and I were thrilled with our personal results with neurofeedback, and we aren't alone. Based on research conducted by Dr. Connie McReynolds at California State University, San Bernardino, neurofeedback has shown promising results in treating PTSD and improving emotional well-being. In a study involving veterans, after twenty hours of neurofeedback, 60 percent reported improvements in their emotional state, and 78 percent experienced a positive state of well-being

> This suggests that neurofeedback can be an effective method for entrepreneurs dealing with unresolved trauma to rewire their brain and enhance their overall mental health.[41]

Another compelling piece of research from Duke University in 2019 demonstrated that neurofeedback could enhance cognitive performance and resilience, which is crucial for entrepreneurs who must maintain high levels of decision-making and creativity under stress.[42]

By embracing neurofeedback, you're not just seeking to mend past wounds; you're stepping towards a future where your mind's fullest potential can be realized, fostering resilience and clarity that propel you beyond the barriers of trauma.

Somatic Experiencing

My initial encounter with Somatic Experiencing (SE) began quite unexpectedly during a course I took on nervous system regulation. Developed by Dr. Peter Levine, SE introduced me to a profound way of healing trauma that was unlike anything I had experienced before. This therapy hinges on a fascinating observation from nature: wild prey animals, though routinely threatened, manage to avoid trauma by naturally regulating and discharging the immense energy related to survival behaviors.[43]

Think of it this way: A deer in the wild is suddenly charged by a lion. It runs and manages to narrowly escape with its life, then immediately shakes it off and goes back to a normal routine. The deer doesn't return to his herd and say, "You'll never guess what just happened to me!" The traumatic event happens, and it's *over*. The deer doesn't harbor trauma for years to come—a trait in human behavior. This natural resilience fascinated and inspired me to explore how we, as humans, could tap into our own innate ability to overcome trauma.

SE focuses less on recounting the distressing memories and more on the bodily sensations these memories evoke. It operates on the principle that trauma disrupts the autonomic nervous system's balance, and recovery is possible by fostering a new way to feel and integrate these bodily sensations.

In the grounding sessions, rather than delving deep into the traumatic events themselves, you learn to gently connect with and understand the physical sensations linked with those memories. This process involves recognizing these sensations, allowing them to surface, and learning to manage them without overwhelming fear or distress.

Through guided physical responses and exercises, SE helps you unlock and release trapped survival energy that has been stored in your body. This approach not only facilitates your journey toward healing but also empowers you with a deeper understanding and appreciation of your body's resilience.

Tension & Trauma Releasing Exercises (TRE)®

While seeing Jenna for craniosacral therapy, she recommended TRE as an effective stress reliever for busy executives, so my husband and I decided to sign up for a class. Before I started on my journey to trauma healing, I had no idea that it is common for business leaders and professionals to carry so much daily work and personal stress (as well as the deeper trauma we are discussing here) that it gets stuck in the body.

Dr. David Berceli is the creator of Tension & Trauma Releasing Exercises (TRE)®, an innovative series of exercises that assist the body in releasing deep muscular patterns of stress, tension, and trauma.

Berceli's inspiration for TRE® arose from observing children in war-torn regions. He noted that children would naturally tremor or shake after experiencing traumatic events, a mechanism he identified as the body's inherent way of releasing tension and stress. Conversely, he observed that adults tended not to exhibit these natural shaking responses, likely due to social conditioning to control or suppress such reactions.

Dr. Berceli then designed TRE® as a series of exercises that encourage this natural shaking process, aiming to help the body let go of deep muscular patterns of stress and tension. The process involves a series of simple exercises that activate these involuntary shakes, helping the body return to a state of balance.

The core idea behind TRE® is that the body holds onto stress and traumatic experiences—sometimes subconsciously—in the form of muscle tension and nervous system imbalances. These retained stresses can lead to various physical and emotional challenges. It involves a series of seven simple and modifiable exercises that help to mildly fatigue the muscles and evoke a natural tremoring response, starting typically from the legs and often spreading throughout the body.

TRE® is used to address a wide array of stress and trauma outcomes. Here are some of the reported benefits:

- **Reduction in anxiety and stress levels.** By releasing deep muscular tension, TRE® can help decrease anxiety and stress.

- **Improved sleep patterns.** Many practitioners report better sleep quality after regular TRE® sessions.
- **Increase in emotional resilience.** The release of physical tension often correlates with emotional releases and greater emotional resilience.
- **Enhancement of overall well-being.** As the body learns to manage stress responses better, overall well-being can improve, including reductions in physical pain and chronic tension.

TRE® is a helpful option to release not only stress from trauma you may be carrying but is also effective for ongoing stress relief and to keep your body in balance. In our first class, I found myself getting frustrated as I couldn't get in tune with the sensations in my body, a necessary step to release stress. With practice, I was able to get the hang of it, and it feels amazing. I now continue to use these exercises a couple of times a week after my workouts to bring my body to a more relaxed state.

Trauma Counseling

In this chapter, I've reviewed EMDR and neurofeedback, two forms of therapy used by a trained trauma therapist. There are others such as family systems therapy, cognitive behavioral therapy, and hypnosis, among others. Recognize that a psychiatrist will most likely want to prescribe medication for anxiety or depression. This happened to me on my first visit, and I politely declined. Though I am not against medication for serious needs, I urge you to proceed with caution here—the United States is the most overprescribed nation on the planet, and it is one of the biggest problems we face with traditional medicine.

The Inspired Performance Program (TIPP)

A good friend of mine, Dr. Don Wood, founder of the Inspired Performance Institute developed the TIPP method to help individuals process and resolve trauma by addressing the body's subconscious response to stress. Though I met Don after my own healing journey had taken place, I had the privilege of visiting his clinic and learning firsthand about his groundbreaking approach to trauma resolution. I was truly impressed with the protocol and have personally known several people who have found profound relief through his work.

The TIPP method works by guiding individuals through a process that helps the brain reprocess and release trauma. It focuses on recalibrating the nervous system and reprogramming the mind to respond more effectively to stressors without becoming overwhelmed by past trauma. The method combines visualization techniques, emotional regulation strategies, and subconscious reprogramming to help people shift out of survival mode and into a state of calm and resilience.

One particularly moving story comes from Rebekah Gregory, a survivor of the Boston Marathon bombing. Rebekah faced years of nightmares and overwhelming anxiety despite trying various therapies and medications. However, after completing the TIPP program, she described a profound sense of clarity and freedom. For the first time in years, she slept peacefully, free from night terrors, and realized that the trauma wasn't something she had to carry with her forever. The TIPP Method empowered her to move forward with confidence and wholeness.

Yoga

For many years, I viewed yoga as just another form of physical exercise—a way to stretch and enhance flexibility. It seemed like a simple activity, and frankly, felt just "too slow" for me. However, my understanding transformed dramatically as I delved deeper into the practice.

I soon realized that yoga was far more than a series of stretches or physical postures; it was a profound journey of connecting the mind and body. Each session on the mat became a time of healing, where I learned to listen to my body's subtle signals and respond with kindness rather than forcing my way through discomfort.

The breath work and meditative aspects of yoga taught me to quiet the persistent noise of stress and anxiety and be present in the moment, fostering a sense of peace that I had not experienced in years. This mind-body connection was pivotal; it allowed me to address not just the symptoms of my stress but the deeper emotional turmoil that fueled it.

> The typical entrepreneur response to trauma we've discussed—shoving it deeply inside—means you have lost the ability to truly quiet your mind and be present in your body.

The typical entrepreneur response to trauma we've discussed—shoving it deeply inside—means you have lost the ability to truly quiet your mind and be present in your body. Yoga offers a sanctuary where you can not only work on your physical well-being but also find mental clarity and emotional balance. It underscores the importance of nurturing not just the body, but also the mind and spirit, to truly live a balanced and fulfilling life.

The profound impact yoga had on my life—both in healing my trauma and maintaining a balanced and regulated nervous system—inspired me to advance my practice. After completing a two hundred–hour course and additional training, this led me to become certified as both a yoga instructor and a trauma-informed yoga practitioner, allowing me to integrate these powerful techniques more fully into my life and coaching work.

Wellness Checks

Regular medical evaluations help identify any physiological issues that may contribute to or exacerbate symptoms of trauma. These wellness checks ensure that any physical health problems, often overlooked in psychological treatment plans, are addressed. For instance, vitamin deficiencies, thyroid problems, or other health issues could mimic or worsen the psychological symptoms associated with trauma.

Other Therapies to Consider

- Acupuncture
- Breathwork and Meditation (discussed in Chapter 10)
- Emotional Freedom Technique (EFT)
- Infrared Sauna
- Massage Therapy
- Qigong
- Tai Chi

I hope you have found these resources and my experience with them helpful. But now, how do you decide where to start? As you have read this list, pick one that piqued your interest and start there. Each modality offers unique benefits and can be combined effectively to support trauma recovery. Accept that not every healing method will resonate with you, and that's okay. It's all about finding what aligns with your unique journey.

As you explore the different therapeutic options available, I encourage you to consult with your doctor and experienced therapists to build a trusted relationship with. They can guide you in choosing the methods that will be most beneficial for your unique situation, ensuring the best outcomes for your health and well-being.

Chapter Reflection

Review the various healing modalities listed in this chapter. What of the trauma therapies would you like to try out to support you in your healing journey? Pick one or two and get started.

- Craniosacral Therapy (CST)
- Eye Movement Desensitization and Reprocessing (EMDR)
- Hormone Replacement Therapy
- Neurofeedback
- Somatic Experiencing
- Tension & Trauma Releasing Exercises (TRE)
- Trauma Counseling
- The Inspired Performance Program (TIPP)
- Yoga

- Wellness Checks
- Acupuncture
- Breathwork and Meditation
- Emotional Freedom Technique (EFT)
- Infrared Sauna
- Massage Therapy
- Qigong
- Tai Chi

Chapter 14

Life Changes for
Sustained Healing

*Whatever life takes away from you, let it go.
When you surrender and let go of your past,
you allow yourself to become fully alive in the
present. Letting go of the past means you can
enjoy the dream that is unfolding right now.*

"When did you get here?" the instructor asked me as I checked into a vinyasa yoga class at CIVANA, a beautiful wellness resort in Arizona. I shared that my husband Graham and I had just arrived that afternoon. "Wow," the instructor commented. "Most people arrive with stress oozing off of them. You are so relaxed and at ease, I thought you had been here for a week!"

What a fabulous compliment to receive—that the healed life I now embrace radiates a newfound relaxed energy. Most driven entrepreneurs, me included, would arrive on vacation hoping to find solace and peace, yet carry the tell-tale signs of modern life's relentless pace: tight shoulders, hurried breaths, and the weight of the world visibly clinging to their shoulders. Add to this a backdrop of unresolved trauma, and the quest for true relaxation becomes even more elusive, making it exceptionally challenging to simply unwind and be at peace.

I share this quick after-story to give you renewed hope and encouragement, demonstrating that healing from trauma is within reach. Despite the fast-paced world you live in that's not going to change, there is a pathway to a life marked by calm and fulfillment.

In this final chapter, let's address how to build resilience and maintain your healing—not just for today but for the rest of your life.

> Emerging from the shadows of past trauma is an accomplishment worth celebrating, but as entrepreneurs and business leaders, your journey doesn't end there.

It's now time to pivot from recovery to resilience—focusing on how to maintain that healing, stay strong amidst the pressures, and ensure you don't slip back into old patterns. We'll talk about:

- How to create intentional life change and success habits to build resilience.
- Specific and simple tools you can incorporate in your day-to-day life to ensure your hard-won healing remains steadfast.

Recharge Your Body, Mind, and Spirit

Picture this: You are sitting at your desk, feeling some fabulous energy to work on an important project. This is going to be a productive day! You then discover something's wrong with your computer....

When you open a program and begin typing, you get the all too familiar buffering symbol telling you your computer is "thinking." You then type in a couple of sentences and wait, then wait some more.... After a significant delay, the words finally appear on the screen in front of you. This goes on for a few frustrating minutes, and you realize your computer is simply bogged down. It is not going to function properly until you reboot it.

Sure enough—after shutting everything down and restarting the computer, everything works fine.

This happens to you and me too. Sometimes we need a "reboot."

You may appear fine on the outside, just like your computer. However, it had way too many programs open and running in the background, causing it to act sluggish and unresponsive. This can happen to you when you have an overload of responsibilities and projects on your plate.

You may start energized and feel like you are crushing it, but the frenzied pace of your life will catch up to you. After a time, you will become tired and sluggish, and find you are no longer performing at your best. I know I have been guilty of taking on too much, and not giving myself the breaks that I need. Can you relate?

We discussed in an earlier chapter how the achiever personality is one that naturally tends to push too hard, often driving yourself beyond your limits pursuing a goal. In taking the steps to heal your past trauma, you are learning how to become more in tune with your body and its needs. However, as an achiever this will be a "watch area" for the future, and that is why it is vital to incorporate time to completely unplug and recharge your body, mind, and spirit.

I have created this discipline in my own life by adding more open space in my weekly calendar and taking regular sabbaticals. A sabbatical is an intentional, extended break from your work that gives you time to rest, recharge, and refocus. Sabbatical comes from the word sabbath, which means "a time of rest." God set the example for us in creation by doing His work and then resting on the sabbath day. He calls you and I to take time for rest too—to stop striving, to be restored and refreshed.

It is not easy, yet taking intentional breaks is critical to your health and well-being. Where do you have these scheduled in your life now? Evaluate your calendar for both work and personal activities to ensure you are taking ample time to rest and renew. Then assess your current stress levels.

Cut Down on Stress

Living with unresolved trauma keeps you stuck in survival mode, with a constantly dysregulated nervous system. Healing your trauma helps bring your system back into balance, achieving homeostasis. Once you've reached this state, it's essential to take steps to maintain it.

To live with less stress, it's important to find a balanced pace. This means slowing down and being mindful of how you spend your time. Don't fall into the trap of working day and night—your body and mind need rest to function optimally.

At the same time, avoid the extremes of inactivity. Staying in bed all day or disengaging from life won't serve you either. Find a rhythm that allows for productivity, but also includes ample time for relaxation, hobbies, and the people you care about.

Examine what's causing stress in your life and be relentless in eliminating those stressors. This might mean setting better boundaries at work, saying no to commitments that overwhelm you, or letting go of relationships that drain your energy. Remember, your well-being comes first. By prioritizing your health and making conscious choices to reduce stress, you create a sustainable lifestyle that supports your healing and growth.

Daily Success Habits to Build Resilience

In your journey toward sustained healing, cultivating resilience is key. Resilience allows you to navigate life's ups and downs with grace and strength, especially after overcoming the shadows of trauma. The secret to building resilience lies in developing habits that support your well-being and empower you to stay on track. By incorporating daily practices that nourish your mind, body, and spirit, you can create a foundation for a balanced and fulfilling life.

One powerful way to build resilience is to start your day with a morning success ritual. I dedicate the first hour of my morning to my well-being, and it's one of the top ways I keep myself healthy and on track. The way you begin your morning sets the tone for the rest of your day, influencing your mindset and energy levels.

Consider creating a routine that includes activities that ground you, inspire you, and prepare you for the challenges ahead. This could be as simple as spending a few moments in gratitude, reflecting on what you're thankful for, and setting positive intentions for the day. A short meditation session can help you center your mind and reduce any lingering anxiety. Incorporating movement, like stretching or a gentle yoga flow, can awaken your body, promote circulation, and boost your mood.

Your morning success ritual is your anchor; it's a way to reclaim your power and set the stage for a successful and resilient day. You can learn more about my morning success ritual on my YouTube channel: @janelle.bruland.

In addition to a morning routine, ongoing engagement in trauma-healing therapies can significantly contribute to resilience. These practices are not just for the initial stages of healing; they are meant to be long-term companions on your journey. Meditation, for example, is a powerful tool that can help you cultivate mindfulness, allowing you to stay present and grounded no matter what life throws your way. Meditation, yoga, and the tension and trauma releasing exercises described in the last chapter are three key practices I use regularly.

Incorporating these habits into your routine supports your ongoing healing and builds a strong foundation of resilience that can sustain you through life's inevitable challenges. Remember, healing is not a destination but a continuous journey.

Your commitment to these practices is a powerful statement to yourself: that your well-being matters, that your past does not define you, and that you have the strength to shape your future. Embrace these habits with consistency and intention, and watch as your resilience grows, empowering you to live a life of purpose and joy.

Looking Forward: Shaping Your Future with Intention

Earlier in the book, you looked at the timeline of your life and you reflected on the defining moments that influenced who you are today. These moments are part of your story, and you can learn from them to create the next chapter of your life with more intention.

Now, it's time to turn your attention to the future. You know that just as you can't relive the past, you can't repeat the decade you're currently in. Whether you're in your twenties, thirties, fifties, or beyond, this decade is unique, and once it's gone, it won't come back. This realization is both sobering and empowering—it's a reminder that you have the opportunity, and indeed the responsibility, to shape the years ahead with intention and clarity.

So, how do you want your current decade to unfold? What do you want to accomplish, both in your business and in your personal life? What kind of leader do you aspire to be? What impact do you want to make? The future is unwritten, and the choices you make today will determine the story you tell tomorrow. This is a powerful moment to pause, reflect, and set a course for the life and leadership legacy you desire.

Start by envisioning your ideal future. What does it look like for you as a healed, whole leader? Who are the people you are surrounded by—both in business and in your personal life? What goals have you achieved, and what kind of culture have you created in your organization? Consider not only your professional aspirations but also your personal ones. What kind of relationships do you want to nurture? How do you want to contribute to your community and leave a lasting impact? What steps can you take to continue enhancing your well-being, both physically and mentally, as a foundational aspect of your success?

It's important to acknowledge that, just as in the past, the future will likely hold its share of unexpected challenges. Life has a way of surprising us, and sometimes those surprises aren't what we had hoped for. But by setting clear intentions and preparing yourself mentally, emotionally, and spiritually, you can navigate these challenges with greater resilience and grace. The inner work you've done to heal your trauma has prepared you to lead from a place of strength and compassion.

As an example, in the middle of writing this book, my dear Dad was diagnosed with terminal cancer, and we lost him in just ten short months. How do you prepare yourself to lay to rest the head of your family—the first man who truly loved you, and who was a consistent, faithful, guiding presence every day of your life?

Through my journey of healing unresolved trauma, I developed a strong mind-body connection, which helped me recognize how my body was reverting to old patterns of dealing with threats and grief—patterns it knew all too well. But I was a different person now, a leader who had chosen to live differently and intentionally. I knew I couldn't go back to my old patterns and habits.

Having walked difficult roads of pain before, I had learned a few things. And I chose to do it differently this time:

- Instead of putting a smile on my face and pretending I was okay, I would be okay with not being okay.
- Instead of closing my heart to avoid the pain, I would stay open and allow myself to feel.

- Instead of ignoring my feelings and sensations, I would embrace it all—the flooding memories, the tears, the heartache, and the joy.

I chose to live by the mantra I shared with you earlier in this book: *Although you can't control the conditions around you, you can control yourself, your attitude, and your response. You can choose a positive mindset and a perspective that leads you forward in the life of significance you are creating, rather than one that holds you back.*

Choose Happy Every Day

Every year, I choose a theme verse to guide me, and one of my favorites comes from Isaiah 43. During my own journey of healing from unresolved trauma, this verse reminded me that I had the power to choose to let go of the pain from my past: *"Forget the former things; do not dwell on the past. See, I am doing a new thing! Now it springs up; do you not perceive it? I am making a way in the wilderness and streams in the wasteland."*[44]

Just like the walls of Jericho came down for good, your past is behind you. It's time to claim the abundant future that lies ahead. It's time to take all the lessons you've learned and live a better story. It's a new day. Are you ready to create the next chapter of your life with intention and purpose?

No matter where you are on your healing journey, remember that you have the power to choose what your life is going to look like. Each day, you decide what kind of day you are going to have. So, let me ask you this: What does your morning look like? Are you getting out of bed each day with joy, ready to embrace the day ahead?

If that got a smirk out of you, listen—I don't always wake up happy and ready to go either. A positive outlook does not always come naturally, especially when making profound changes in your life. That's okay; you're human after all. But here's the thing: You can choose to be happy, hopeful, and at peace, or you can choose otherwise. This choice is yours—*every single day.*

Start today. Choose to make every day one of peace, hope, and overflowing joy. Cultivate such positive thoughts that they pour out of you and touch everyone around you.

> Begin each day with intention. For me, that means starting my day with God and my morning success ritual. I take a few minutes to check in with myself, sensing how I am feeling physically, mentally, emotionally, and spiritually. Whatever comes up, I welcome it, spend some time with it, and then surrender it. Then I intentionally change my mindset as we talked about in Chapter 9. I focus on the good in my life and choose to be joyful and grateful.

Remember, each day is a new opportunity to choose how you respond to the world.

- Decide that it is going to be a great day.
- Decide to have an optimistic attitude.
- Decide to look forward to your future with hope.
- Decide to be grateful for everything you have.

As you move forward, remember you don't have to continue living the way your story has been written so far. You have the pen, and you have the power to write a better story.

> Imagine your new chapter, your new life—one filled with joy, peace, and purpose. You are no longer someone who is weighed down by past pain, worry, or regret, but one who lives each day fully, with an open heart and a clear mind.

The path to happiness and fulfillment is there for you to step into. Decide every morning what kind of day you want to have, and then live it. Choose happy, every day.

Conclusion

My friend, no matter what you have endured, know this: you have the power to take back control of your life. There is hope, even in the moments when hope feels distant. The path to happiness, inner peace, and renewed confidence is within your reach. Imagine stepping into a new level of leadership, one that is deeply rooted in authenticity and clarity. It's time to release yourself fully from the shadows of your past and open up to the limitless possibilities of your future.

Throughout this book, we have taken this journey together. In Part One, we explored the hidden impact of unresolved trauma and how it often remains concealed, even behind the facade of entrepreneurial success. We acknowledged the frustration of realizing that the same drive and determination that helped you succeed in business cannot heal the wounds of your past. But as we've discovered, feeling powerless is not the end of the story. With the right tools and understanding, you can reclaim your power.

In Part Two, I shared the practical tools and techniques that have transformed my life, offering a step-by-step approach to healing. You've learned to connect more deeply with your body and understand how it protects you. More importantly, you've discovered how to let go of what no longer serves you, making room for healing and growth.

As you move forward, remember that healing is not just a one-time event but a continuous process. The changes you make in your daily life will be your compass, guiding you toward resilience and lasting peace.

This book is your roadmap, and, with it, you have everything you need to sustain your healing and thrive. You've already taken the most important step by choosing to embark on this journey. Now, continue to embrace these practices and build a life of happiness, fulfillment, and unshakeable strength. Your way back to happiness is not just possible—it's already unfolding.

Resources To Help You

YOUR WAY BACK TO HAPPY BOOK

This is just the beginning of your journey back to happy. Dive deeper into the concepts in this book and access valuable resources, including guided meditations, journaling prompts, and more, at www.yourwaybacktohappy.com

JOIN IMPACT MASTERMIND

Picture yourself surrounded by a community of like-minded leaders, achieving your goals while experiencing deep fulfillment and balance. That's the power of IMPACT. Are you ready to unlock your full potential and experience the transformative power of living an intentional life?

BOOK JANELLE

Ignite your audience with Janelle Bruland' s powerful message of resilience, leadership, and creating a life of impact. Book Janelle to speak at your next event and empower yourself and your team to achieve extraordinary results while prioritizing well- being and joy.

THE SUCCESS LIE BOOK

The Success Lie, challenges the myth that you have to sacrifice your well- being to achieve success. It' s a guide to overcoming overwhelm, redefining success on your own terms, and creating a life of true significance.

INTENTIONAL LEADERSHIP SHOW

Tune in to the Intentional Leadership Show and discover how to lead with greater purpose, impact, and joy. Each episode is designed to empower you with practical strategies and inspiring insights to elevate your leadership and create a thriving team culture. Watch now: www. youtube. com/@janelle. bruland

For questions about any of these strategies or investments please contact us at: www.janellebruland.com

Endnotes

1. Peter A. Levine (Berkeley, Calif.: North Atlantic Books, 1997).
2. World Health Organization, "Post-Traumatic Stress Disorder," World Health Organization, May 24, 2024, https://www.who.int/news-room/fact-sheets/detail/post-traumatic-stress-disorder#:~:text=Around%2070%25%20of%20people%20globally.
3. World Health Organization, "Mental Health in the Workplace," World Health Organization, accessed November 10, 2024, https://www.who.int/teams/mental-health-and-substance-use/promotion-prevention/mental-health-in-the-workplace.
4. Vivek Murthy, "Work and the Loneliness Epidemic," *Harvard Business Review*, September 26, 2017, https://hbr.org/2017/09/work-and-the-loneliness-epidemic.
5. Jeff Kauflin, "Forget 'Crushing It,' Startup Founders Open Up About Mental Health Problems," *Forbes*, October 25, 2023, https://www.forbes.com/sites/jeffkauflin/2023/10/25/forget-crushing-it-startup-founders-open-up-about-mental-health-problems/#:~:text=Thirty%2Deight%20percent%20have%20experienced.
6. M. E. Seligman and S. F. Maier, "Failure to Escape Traumatic Shock," *Journal of Experimental Psychology* 74, no. 1 (1967):1–9, http://dx.doi.org/10.1037/h0024514.
7. Benjamin Suarez-Jimenez, "Researchers Reveal How Trauma Changes the Brain," University of Rochester Medical Center

Newsroom, December 7, 2022, https://www.urmc.rochester.edu/news/publications/neuroscience/researchers-reveal-how-trauma-changes-the-brain.

[8] Bremner, J Douglas. "Traumatic stress: effects on the brain." Dialogues in clinical neuroscience vol. 8,4 (2006): 445-61. doi:10.31887/DCNS.2006.8.4/jbremner

[9] New Living Translation Bible (NLT). Gupta PhD, Nijay K., Tyndale House Publishers, 2021, 1 Peter 5:8. Accessed 25 November 2024.

[10] Hochgerner, H., Singh, S., Tibi, M. *et al.* Neuronal types in the mouse amygdala and their transcriptional response to fear conditioning. *Nat Neurosci* **26**, 2237–2249 (2023). https://doi.org/10.1038/s41593-023-01469-3.

[11] Stephen Maren and Andrew Holmes, "Stress and Fear Extinction," *Neuropsychopharmacology* 41 (2016): 58–79, https://doi.org/10.1038/npp.2015.180.

[12] Jonathan P. Fadok, "Taming the Amygdala in PTSD," *Psychology Today*, March 19, 2019, https://www.psychologytoday.com/us/blog/cant-stress-this-enough/202403/taming-the-amygdala-in-ptsd.

[13] Mary M. Volcheck et al., "Central Sensitization, Chronic Pain, and Other Symptoms: Better Understanding, Better Management," *Cleveland Clinic Journal of Medicine* 90, no. 4 (2023): 24–54, https://doi.org/10.3949/ccjm.90a.22019.

[14] Dana Sparks, "Chronic Stress Can Wreak Havoc on Your Mind and Body," Mayo Clinic News Network, July 12, 2021, https://newsnetwork.mayoclinic.org/discussion/chronic-stress-can-wreak-havoc-on-your-mind-and-body/.

[15] American Psychological Association, "Mindfulness Meditation: A Research-Proven Way to Reduce Stress," American Psychological Association, October 30, 2019, https://www.apa.org/topics/mindfulness/meditation.

16 "Mind over matter." Merriam-Webster.com Dictionary, Merriam-Webster, https://www.merriam-webster.com/dictionary/mind%20over%20matter. Accessed 21 Nov. 2024.

17 Bruce S. McEwen, "Neurobiological and Systemic Effects of Chronic Stress," *Chronic Stress* 1 (2017), https://doi.org/10.1177/2470547017692328.

18 Megan Call, "Neuroplasticity: How to Use Your Brain's Malleability to Improve Your Well-Being," Health—University of Utah, August 8, 2019, https://accelerate.uofuhealth.utah.edu/resilience/neuroplasticity-how-to-use-your-brain-s-malleability-to-improve-your-well-being.

19 Michael M. Merzenich, Thomas M. Van Vleet, and Mor Nahum, "Brain Plasticity-Based Therapeutics," *Frontiers in Human Neuroscience* 8 (2014): 1–16, https://doi.org/10.3389/fnhum.2014.00385.

20 Norman Doidge, *The Brain That Changes Itself: Stories of Personal Triumph From the Frontiers of Brain Science.* (New York: Penguin Life, 2007).

21 Caroline Leaf et al., "Habit Formation and Automaticity: Psychoneurobiological Correlates of Gamma Activity," *NeuroRegulation* 11, no. 1 (2024): 2–24, https://doi.org/10.15540/nr.11.1.2.

22 Christoph Kraus et al., "Serotonin and Neuroplasticity—Links Between Molecular, Functional and Structural Pathophysiology in Depression," *Neuroscience & Biobehavioral Reviews* 77 (June): 317–26, https://doi.org/10.1016/j.neubiorev.2017.03.007.

23 Brigid Schulte, "Harvard Neuroscientist: Meditation Not Only Reduces Stress, Here's How It Changes Your Brain," *The Washington Post*, May 26, 2015, https://washingtonpost.com/news/inspired-life/wp/2015/05/26/harvard-neuroscientist-meditation-not-only-reduces-stress-it-literally-changes-your-brain/; Sara W. Lazar et al., "Meditation Experience Is Associated with

Increased Cortical Thickness," *NeuroReport* 16 (17): 1893–97, https://www.ncbi.nlm.nih.gov/pmc/articles/PMC1361002/.

[24] American Heart Association, "Meditation to Boost Health and Well-Being," Heart.org, American Heart Association, last reviewed January 25, 2024, https://www.heart.org/en/healthy-living/healthy-lifestyle/mental-health-and-wellbeing/meditation-to-boost-health-and-wellbeing; American Heart Association, "Mindfulness Shows Promise as an Effective Intervention to Lower Blood Pressure." Heart.org, American Heart Association, November 6, 2022, https://newsroom.heart.org/news/mindfulness-shows-promise-as-an-effective-intervention-to-lower-blood-pressure.

[25] Jennifer Todd and Jane E. Aspell, "Mindfulness, Interoception, and the Body." *Brain Sciences* 12, no. 6 (2022): 696, https://doi.org/10.3390/brainsci12060696.

[26] Ran Wu et al., "Brief Mindfulness Meditation Improves Emotion Processing," *Frontiers in Neuroscience* 13 (2019), https://doi.org/10.3389/fnins.2019.01074.

[27] Yuval Engel, Anusha Ramesh, and Nick Steiner, "Powered by Compassion: The Effect of Loving-Kindness Meditation on Entrepreneurs' Sustainable Decision-Making," *Journal of Business Venturing* 35, no. 6 (2020): 105986, https://doi.org/10.1016/j.jbusvent.2019.105986.

[28] New Living Translation Bible (NLT). Gupta PhD, Nijay K., Tyndale House Publishers, 2021, Psalm 119:97. Accessed 25 November 2024.

[29] New Living Translation Bible (NLT). Gupta PhD, Nijay K., Tyndale House Publishers, 2021, Romans 12:2. Accessed 25 November 2024.

[30] Melis Yilmaz Balban et al., "Brief Structured Respiration Practices Enhance Mood and Reduce Physiological Arousal." *Cell Reports Medicine* 4, no. 1 (2023), https://doi.org/10.1016/j.xcrm.2022.100895.

[31] Lacey Whited, Muhammad F. Hashmi, and Derrel D. Graham, *Abnormal Respirations* (Treasure Island, FL: StatPearls Publishing, 2023), https://www.ncbi.nlm.nih.gov/books/NBK470309/.

[32] Jennifer N. Morey et al., "Current Directions in Stress and Human Immune Function," *Current Opinion in Psychology* 5 (2015): 13–17, https://doi.org/10.1016/j.copsyc.2015.03.007; Mohammed Iddir et al., "Strengthening the Immune System and Reducing Inflammation and Oxidative Stress through Diet and Nutrition: Considerations during the COVID-19 Crisis," *Nutrients* 12, no. 6 (2020): 1562, https://doi.org/10.3390/nu12061562.

[33] Bessel A. van der Kolk, *The Body Keeps the Score: Brain, Mind, and Body in the Healing of Trauma* (New York, New York: Penguin Books, 2015).

[34] "Stress in America 2023: A Nation Recovering From Collective Trauma," Data set, PsycEXTRA Dataset, January 1, 2023, https://doi.org/10.1037/e505462023-001.

[35] John P. Capitanio, "Personality and Disease," *Brain, Behavior, and Immunity* 22, no. 5 (2008): 647–50, https://doi.org/10.1016/j.bbi.2008.02.002.

[36] Uma Naidoo, *This Is Your Brain on Food: An Indispensable Guide to the Surprising Foods that Fight Depression, Anxiety, PTSD, OCD, ADHD, and More* (New York, New York: Little, Brown Spark, 2020).

[37] Matthew Walker, *Why We Sleep: Unlocking the Power of Sleep and Dreams* (New York, New York: Scribner, 2018).

[38] Matthew Walker, *Why We Sleep: Unlocking the Power of Sleep and Dreams* (New York, New York: Scribner, 2018).

[39] Heidemarie Haller, Gustav Dobos, and Holger Cramer, "The Use and Benefits of Craniosacral Therapy in Primary Health Care: A Prospective Cohort Study," *Complementary Therapies in Medicine* 58 (2021): 102702, https://doi.org/10.1016/j.ctim.2021.102702.

[40] Helen P. A. Driessen, "Eye Movement Desensitization and Reprocessing (EMDR) Treatment in the Medical

Setting: A Systematic Review," *European Journal of Psychotraumatology* 15, no. 1 (2024): 2341577, https://ncbi.nlm.nih.gov/pmc/articles/PMC11097707/.

[41] Connie McReynolds, Jodi Bell, and Tina M. Lincourt, "Neurofeedback: A Noninvasive Treatment for Symptoms of Posttraumatic Stress Disorder in Veterans," *NeuroRegulation* 4, no. 3–4 (2017): 114–24, https://doi.org/10.15540/nr.4.3-4.114.

[42] Katherine E. MacDuffie et al., "Single Session Real-Time fMRI Neurofeedback Has a Lasting Impact on Cognitive Behavioral Therapy Strategies," *NeuroImage: Clinical* 19 (2018): 868–75, https://scholars.duke.edu/publication/1325052.

[43] Levine, *Waking the Tiger: Healing Trauma.*

[44] New Living Translation Bible (NLT). Gupta PhD, Nijay K., Tyndale House Publishers, 2021, Isaiah 43: 18-19. Accessed 25 November 2024.

Acknowledgments

Writing this book was one of the most personal and challenging endeavors I have ever undertaken. It's one thing to write about leadership, strategy, and success—things I've spent a lifetime studying and teaching. It's another thing entirely to be vulnerable about the unseen struggles that have shaped me, the past wounds I once buried, and the healing journey that ultimately transformed my life.

I never set out to write *Your Way Back to Happy*. In fact, for a long time, I didn't even recognize how much I needed my own healing. But in the midst of that journey, I woke up one night with the entire outline of this book in my mind—like a divine download that I could not ignore. I knew in that moment that God was calling me to share this story, to help others find the path I had so desperately sought. To the entrepreneurs, leaders, and high achievers who are exhausted from carrying the unseen weight of their past, this book is for you. My greatest hope is that it serves as a guide to freedom, to joy, and to a new way of living and leading.

A book like this is never a solo endeavor. It is the culmination of wisdom gathered over a lifetime from mentors, colleagues, friends, and family who have shaped me in profound ways.

To my family, children, and grandchildren, the greatest joys of my life—thank you for your love, your laughter, and for always grounding me in what matters most. A special thank you to my husband, Graham—my rock, my greatest supporter, and my best friend. Your belief in me has never wavered, even when I questioned myself. Thank you for listening, encouraging, and holding space for me through every high and low. I truly could not have done this without you.

To my team and the incredible clients I have had the privilege of working with over the years—your trust and partnership have meant everything. To those in *IMPACT Mastermind* and my *Success Life* coaching programs, your hunger for growth and transformation is what drives me to continue this work. You inspire me daily.

A special thank you to my agent, Ken Anderson, and to Debby Englander and the amazing team at Point Hill Press— your belief in this book and dedication to bringing it to life mean the world. I'm also deeply grateful to my superstar marketing team—your expertise, creativity, and hard work made this journey successful and a ton of fun.

And finally, above all else, I give thanks to God—who not only gave me the gifts and passion to lead but also the endurance to heal, to write, and to complete this work. This book exists because of His grace, and to Him be all the glory.

About the Author

Janelle Bruland is an award-winning entrepreneur, speaker, and executive leadership coach who inspires others to live impactful and intentional lives. She is the author of *The Success Lie: 5 Simple Truths to Overcome Overwhelm and Achieve Peace of Mind* described as a "Must-Read Book for Those Seeking Success" by *Success* magazine and winning praise from bestselling authors Mel Robbins and Hal Elrod, as well as CEOs Tom Ziglar (Ziglar Inc), Mark Cole (The John Maxwell Company), and Dan Sullivan (The Strategic Coach).

Janelle and her partner in life and business, Graham Youtsey, are the founders of Legacy Leader, a leadership development company, and IMPACT—the premier community for driven, faith-based entrepreneurs changing the world. She is also founder, former president, and CEO of Management Services Northwest (MSNW), a company she grew from a start-up in her living room to a multi-state-industry leader, named one of the "Fastest-Growing Private Companies in America" by *Inc.* magazine nine times.

As a contributor to leading publications including *Thrive Global, Market Watch,* and *Forbes,* and through her podcast *Intentional Leadership,* Janelle draws from extensive experience to arm people with the mindset, strategies, and tools that are essential to lead themselves and others to better outcomes. She pursued certifications in mindfulness, meditation, and trauma-informed yoga, yet another tool she uses to teach people to overcome their own challenges. With a genuine heart, Janelle helps leaders fortify their minds so they are best equipped to overcome unresolved trauma and embrace peace and balance in their lives.

Janelle is a loving mother of five, a fun and devoted nana, and lives with her family in Birch Bay, Washington.